THE MIRACLE OF
THE SACRED SHROUD OF TURIN

It is believed to be the burial cloth of Jesus. On its fine linen surface appears the image of a man bearing the wounds of crucifixion . . . a photographic image produced by a process totally unknown to the ancient world!

What new theories can science offer to explain this miraculous phenomenon?

The Shroud of Turin is but one of the intriguing clues to the life of Jesus which you will discover . . .

IN SEARCH OF HISTORIC JESUS

IN SEARCH OF HISTORIC JESUS

starring
JOHN RUBINSTEIN
JOHN ANDERSON
NEHEMIAH PERSOFF
BRAD CRANDALL

Screenplay by
Malvin Wald & Jack Jacobs

Produced by
Charles E. Sellier, Jr.
& James L. Conway

Directed by
Henning Schellerup

IN SEARCH OF HISTORIC JESUS

LEE RODDY
AND
CHARLES E. SELLIER JR.

TORONTO · BANTAM BOOKS · LONDON
NEW YORK

The authors and publisher wish
to express their grateful
appreciation to Robert Starling
and Julia Mair for their extensive
research assistance in the
preparation of this book.

IN SEARCH OF HISTORIC JESUS
A Bantam Book / December 1979

ISBN: 0-553-13588-0

Published simultaneously in the United States and Canada

*Bantam Books are published by Bantam Books, Inc. Its trade-
mark, consisting of the words "Bantam Books" and the por-
trayal of a bantam, is Registered in U.S. Patent and Trademark
Office and in other countries. Marca Registrada. Bantam
Books, Inc., 666 Fifth Avenue, New York, New York 10019.*

PRINTED IN THE UNITED STATES OF AMERICA

CONTENTS

1. The Quest Begins   1
2. The Bible as an Historical Document   11
3. Messianic Prophecies and the Story of the Nativity   21
4. The Mystery of Where Jesus Spent His Boyhood   36
5. The Eighteen Missing Years in Jesus' Life   44
6. Historical Background of the Gospels   52
7. Conflicts over Jesus' Ministry   66
8. The Final Days of Jesus' Life   80
9. Jesus' Trial   88
10. The Road to Calvary   98
11. The Burial and Resurrection of Jesus   108
12. Echoes from an Empty Tomb   115
13. A Secret in an Italian Attic   125
14. The History and Mystery of the Shroud   136
15. Testimony from a 2,000-Year-Old Cloth   148
16. Could Jesus Have Visited the Americas?   158
    Notes   169
    Bibliography   173

IN SEARCH
OF
HISTORIC JESUS

1

THE QUEST BEGINS

It had been a hard week for the four Roman soldiers standing guard outside a Jerusalem tomb. They would be glad when the dawn came, for then it would all be over and everyone could go home. Things would settle down to normal and the name of the dead man in the tomb would soon be forgotten.

He had been called Jesus of Nazareth and had been about thirty-three years old when he died on a Roman cross Friday afternoon, nearly three days before. Jesus would probably still have been alive if he had stayed up north in Galilee, where he had been teaching for about three years except for periodic trips here to Judea.

This Jesus was also said to have been a healer and even to have raised a couple of people from the dead. The Roman soldiers didn't believe this was so; nobody came back from the dead. Still, the high priests who had gotten the Roman governor to crucify Jesus seemed concerned that his disciples would steal his body and claim Jesus had risen from the dead. There was some report that Jesus had said he would come back to life on the third day. So the soldiers had been assigned by Governor Pontius Pilate to guard the tomb.

It was a boring task. Back and forth, back and forth, meeting and passing each other, hour after hour!

But that was the way it was for a Roman occupation army; there were always wearisome duties like pacing in front of a rock-hewn tomb cut into a hillside outside of Jerusalem's walls. It wasn't so bad under the full moon here in the garden, where some rich man had given his own intended tomb to the teacher from Galilee. It was nicer than some of the other guard duties the Romans had endured.

And it was a quiet night. The Jews were all indoors. It was their Sabbath, the day of rest that their one God had commanded them to observe thousands of years ago. It was also the Jewish holiday called Passover. That had something to do with a story the Jews told about their great lawgiver, Moses, who had led them out of Egyptian slavery. According to the story, the Hebrews (as the Jews were then called) had been slaves in Egypt for about four hundred years. Then, after a series of plagues brought by their God upon the Egyptians, there had been one night when the Angel of Death had struck down every first-born person and animal of the Egyptians, leaving the Hebrews unharmed. The Pharaoh had thrown the Hebrews out of the land. Their descendants had never forgotten how they had been freed from bondage, and so each spring, at the full moon following the rains, they held a Passover observance.

Passover was the time when the Jews were most likely to cause trouble for the Romans, and that was why Governor Pontius Pilate was in Jerusalem to maintain order. The Jews never could seem to understand that they were a conquered people and that Rome ruled the world, including this tiny little patch of desert and mountains.

It was ironic to the Roman soldiers guarding the tomb that this small nation of Jews would still celebrate their Passover as a time of freedom when they had rarely been free since they had fled Egypt.

Of course, there had been some periods of home rule. The Hebrews had followed Moses to the land promised their ancestor, Abraham. His grandson, Jacob, or Israel, as he was later known, had had twelve sons.

These had become the Twelve Tribes of Israel. Under Moses' successor, Joshua, the tribes had dispossessed the Canaanites and other indigenous peoples of their land. The Hebrews had reached their greatest glory under King David, who had united the tribes into a monarchy about a thousand years before.

It was then that the Hebrews formed the idea that one of David's descendants would always sit on the throne. The Jewish belief that their God had promised this to David still motivated the people to expect the coming of the anointed one, or *Messiah,* which was the Hebrew word for "anointed." The Greek word was *Christ.* It was derived from the ancient Hebraic ritual of anointing the head of the priest or king with oil, as a sign that he had been chosen by God.

Jesus had been crucified because many of the people had begun to believe that he was their long-awaited Messiah, and because this made the Jewish political leaders view him as a threat to their authority. They had conspired to have the governor execute him, for the Jews didn't have the authority to render a sentence of capital punishment on their own.

Obviously, Jesus wasn't the Jewish Messiah! He lay dead behind the great rolling stone that covered the entrance of the tomb. The people were still prisoners in their own land, as they had been so often through the centuries. And still they celebrated Passover.

Palestine, as the Greek historian Herodotus had called the Promised Land, had almost never been free since the throne had been lost by David's grandson and the area had been divided into Israel in the north and Judea in the south. The Assyrians had deported ten tribes of Hebrews a thousand miles or more beyond the great Sahara Desert. These tribes had vanished into oblivion. About a century later, the Babylonians had exiled the two remaining tribes from the south. Eventually, some of the tribe of Judah had returned. From that time, they were no longer called Hebrews, but Jews, for their ancestor, Judah.

They continued to celebrate their Passover down through those troubled years, even under repeated military occupation. The main forces had come from Greece, which had conquered much of the known world, including Palestine, about three hundred years ago. The Romans had succeeded them as military rulers when Pompey took Jerusalem, after only a brief period during which the Jews enjoyed home rule under the Maccabees. Since then, under Herod the King, his sons, or Roman governors or procurators, Rome had ruled the Jews. Right now, Herod Antipas governed in Galilee and Pilate in Judea. No wonder the Jews longed for a Messiah!

But, though century after century had gone by, he still hadn't arrived. The Romans had been in Jerusalem for about ninety years now. They expected to stay much longer, no matter how much the Jews longed for their Messiah.

In their sacred book, the *Torah,* the Jews could read about their God's own promise that the Messiah would come. This promise had often been reaffirmed by the Jewish prophets, who were said to speak as the representatives of God. But the last prophet in their Scriptures had spoken about five hundred years ago. That was a long time for a people sighing under military occupation forces.

And during this time the people had often been disappointed. The latest messianic expectations had arisen as a result of Jesus' career, but now that he lay dead beyond the door of the tomb, they too had been shattered. He had been hastily buried on Friday afternoon after being removed from the cross. Jewish law forbade even burial on the Sabbath, so some men named Nicodemus and Joseph of Arimathea had hastily wrapped the corpse and placed it in the tomb before sundown, when the Sabbath began.

The body lay face up on a stone bench in a carved niche, the spot that Joseph of Arimathea had intended would eventually be his own burial place. The whole tomb was wrapped in soft darkness because of the ponderous stone that had been rolled into place to close the entrance. Pilate's own signet ring had been pressed into the seals, which had now hardened into place. The tomb was inviolate. The soldiers continued their pacing, stifling yawns and waiting for the approach of dawn.

The hopes of many people lay buried with Jesus of Nazareth. After all, hadn't he given signs with his miracles? And, of course, his disciples and the women who had followed him from Galilee to Judea had expected that great things would occur when Jesus got to Jerusalem this time. Now it was all over. Jesus had been dead for thirty-six hours or so. Everyone had gone home except the guards, and they would head for their barracks at the end of the watch.

Life would resume its normal pace at the break of day. The Jews would continue their eight-day celebration of Passover and the Feast of Unleavened Bread. The women would come to finish preparing Jesus' body for a proper burial. The Jews would continue hoping for their Messiah. And the Romans would continue to rule as an occupation army under Pilate in Judea, and under Herod Antipas, called the Tetrarch, who governed in Galilee to the north.

That was the situation just before dawn on the third day after Jesus was crucified.

The youngest of the four Roman soldiers glanced at the eastern sky beyond the Mount of Olives and decided to take a break. He obtained permission from the centurion with the crested helmet, who also motioned for a second legionnaire to rest. The centurion and one other soldier in bright red tunic and leather greaves continued their pacing.

The youngest guard yawned widely, lowered his iron-tipped lance and curved shield, and walked wearily to the warming fire. He nodded to his comrade-in-arms, who was settling down by the fire with a long, weary sigh. But before the young soldier could lay down his lance and shield, something happened.

At first it felt like a vibration in his Roman military sandal-boots. Then it became a rumble. He leaped up, automatically shoving his curved shield out with his left hand and tipping the iron-pointed lance toward the place from which the sound seemed to originate.

His companion also jumped up, scattering the warming fire's coals with the blunt end of his spear. In a hoarse whisper he asked, "What's that?"

The young Roman didn't answer. The rumbling had increased so much that he couldn't keep his balance. He dropped his shield with a clatter and frantically grabbed for a bush to steady himself.

The other two soldiers had stopped their pacing and stood with legs spread and braced, spears tilted toward the limestone cave, where the sound seemed to be loudest.

The terror of the earthquake was increased by a strange glow that was coming—impossible as it seemed —from behind the stone covering the entrance to the grave.

Inside the tomb, the cloth-wrapped body of Jesus was tinged with a soft, white light. The linen shroud covering the body was pulsating at a rapidly increasing pace. In spite of the darkness, the burial cloth was becoming visible and taking shape as a white length of purest light—light so strong that it totally illuminated the tomb.

Suddenly, the light exploded outward with such intensity that it burst the sealed entrance of the tomb, as though the stone hadn't been there at all.

Outside, in the garden, the shadows were washed away in a blinding flash. Small birds were startled and flushed from their roosts. They fluttered awkwardly in the direction of the retreating darkness, and vanished into the distance. The soldiers threw their hands or forearms across their eyes and reeled backward, stumbling and falling as a result of the momentary blindness that engulfed them.

The sound of the earthquake grew deeper still. The guards heard the great round stone at the burial entrance begin to move. The governor's seals cracked sharply. Then the stone's huge weight ponderously inched away from the broken seals, rolling heavily aside in the trough cut at the bottom of the tomb's entrance.

Blinded by the painful intensity of the light, the soldiers had not seen the inside of the tomb. But when the immense stone had rolled clear, leaving an unobstructed view of the interior of the tomb, there could be no doubt about what had happened.

The youngest soldier's fears overcame his training. He groped blindly for the path from the garden and, screaming in terror, stumbled from the scene. His companions, overcome with the terror of the unknown, shamelessly followed, yelling and sobbing.

They gained the entrance to the garden and lurched toward their camp, north of the city's walls. But already each man's mind was instinctively inventing a plausible excuse for having vacated his post.

Inside the garden, the earthquake had subsided. Although the antechamber retained a phosphorescent glow, the darkness had regained control of the tomb.

But it was obvious that something remarkable had happened.

Jesus' body was not there.

The tomb was empty.

All that remained were the burial linens.

The total significance of this event would not be known for nearly twenty centuries. But the controversy and mystery about Jesus of Nazareth began immediately that spring morning in Jerusalem. After two thousand years, the controversy still remains.

Who was this Jesus, really?

Was he, as his disciples claimed, the promised Messiah and the Son of God?

Did Jesus really rise from the dead, as his followers claimed, or did his disciples steal the body from the tomb while the guards slept, as the Jewish officials claimed?

For two millennia, the primary source of information about Jesus has been the twenty-seven books of the New Testament. For Christians, who believe what these books say about Jesus, the New Testament is an essential part of the Bible.

The majority of Jews, however, do not accept any of the New Testament as part of the thirty-nine books of their Bible. They consider their Scriptures complete without the four Gospels and the epistles that constitute the New Testament. Judaism has always rejected the assertion that Jesus was anything more than a good man and a teacher. It denies that God, being one and indivisible, could have had a son.

So, for two thousand years, the controversy has raged about Jesus of Nazareth. Few people, it seems, have no opinion about him. But what is the authority for their belief?

The purpose of this book is to explore the resources available to modern historiography and to compare and combine them with what the Gospels record—in effect, to go in search of the historic Jesus.

Two views of Jesus have been commonly held:

1. *The Jesus of faith.* This is the view held by those who believe that Jesus was divine, and who require no other proof of his divinity beyond the New Testament.

2. *The Jesus of temporal or secular history.* This is the view held by those who do not believe that Jesus was divine, and who reject the authority of the Gospels as proof of his divinity.

In order to begin to put this age-old controversy into perspective, we have to ask a number of questions:

What is the non-New Testament documentation that Jesus actually lived and died?

How should we interpret the references and allusions to Jesus by writers who lived during or around the time of the crucifixion, such as the famed Jewish historian Josephus or the first-century pagan chroniclers Suetonius, Tacitus, and Pliny?

Is it possible that the cuneiform tablets of ancient astrologers could have recorded such heavenly phenomena as the Star of Bethlehem? Can the mysterious darkness at noon which the Gospels associated with Jesus' hour of death on the cross be corroborated by the strange mid-day blackness coming about the year of Jesus' death which the astronomer Thallus recorded? Can modern astronomical methods prove the occurrence of an eclipse at the time Jesus died?

There are many apocryphal accounts of the life of Jesus—writings that may once have been a part of the Bible but are no longer considered to be genuine. Is it possible that some of the material from these "hidden books" is worth considering in our search for the historic Jesus?

What about the strange legends of ancient peoples, as far off as Alaska and the Pacific Islands, that a white, bearded God would return to them, even as Jesus of Nazareth had promised to return? The first white explorers on the American continent had been startled to find that some highly advanced Indian civilizations practiced religious rites resembling those of the arriving Christians. What was the origin of such rites?

Is there any possible piece of physical evidence still in existence that might confirm the account of the Gospels that, having endured the agony of the cross, Jesus was resurrected? Would the so-called Shroud of Turin have anything to offer in our quest for the historic Jesus?

What about the Dead Sea Scrolls and the discovery at Nag Hammadi?

There are letters reputedly from Pontius Pilate to Emperor Tiberius Caesar mentioning Jesus' trial. Are they authentic?

What about legends that claim Jesus went to Britain, Greece, Egypt, India, Kashmir, Persia, and various other countries? After all, the Gospels are silent about Jesus' exact whereabouts from the age of twelve to about thirty. Where was Jesus during those eighteen years?

Do non-biblical texts, such as the Book of Mormon, that claim that the resurrected Jesus appeared to others besides those mentioned in the New Testament, shed any light on the mystery?

To be fair in the search for the historic Jesus, denominational lines must be crossed. Investigation should include a look at viewpoints held by Jews, Catholics, Protestants, Mormons, and others who hold differing opinions. An examination must be made of pagan writings, as well as of oral and written legends that cross cultural boundaries.

Everything that might bear on our quest for knowledge about the historical Jesus must be examined with an open mind, as a detective considers all pieces of evidence, all possible clues in a mystery.

Our examination must, however, be conducted scientifically if it is to result in genuine historical knowledge. If data examined in our search does not stand up to scientific scrutiny, it should be rejected. Our approach must be impartial.

2

THE BIBLE AS AN HISTORICAL DOCUMENT

Besides the Bible, we will use many resources in our search for the historic Jesus, such as the Nag Hammadi Manuscripts, the Dead Sea Scrolls, the Apocrypha, and legends and myths from other cultures. And, of course, we will make use of such sciences as archaeology and astronomy in various ways.

Many people think that outside of the Bible there is little information about Jesus, but in fact there is an abundance of data. Some of it is of doubtful authenticity, but much of it offers new insights into the most fascinating figure in history.

However, since the Bible is the primary source of information about Jesus, we should begin our search there. We must first consider what the Bible is, how it came to be, and how reliable it is as an historical document.

The word Bible is derived through Latin from *biblia,* the plural of the Greek word for "book." In its Greek form, the word may have been used to refer to the books which had already begun to be considered canonical—sacred or officially approved—as early as the second century AD. Before that, the preferred term was Scripture or Holy Scriptures, which contained The

Law, The Writings, and The Prophets as subdivisions. The Scriptures consisted exclusively of the books of the Old Testament until after Jesus' time, when the Christians (those who follow Christ's teachings) added the New Testament to the canon of what the Jews already possessed.

The principal groups using the Bible (Jews, Catholics, and Protestants) consider that the document is the Word of God and that the guidelines it contains are those by which people may live uprightly. Yet the three groups cited above disagree on what the Bible contains. The Jews originally had twenty-four books, of which some material was rejected and some expanded until the thirty-nine officially approved books of the Old Testament had arrived at their final canonical version.

Jews consider their sacred Scriptures to be complete without what Catholics and Protestants call the New Testament. To Catholics and Protestants, the Bible is a compendium of the Old Testament of the Jews and the New Testament.

Protestants, who grew out of the Reformation in the sixteenth century, have omitted some books from the Old Testament which Catholics consider canonical: Judith, Tobit, and the two Maccabees, for example. Although Jews and Protestants consider them apocryphal, the famed Protestant Bible known as the King James Version contained these "hidden" books until 1628.

As with the Jewish canon, the Catholic choice of which books to designate as official was made by men who believed their decisions were divinely guided. The Protestants later made the same claim in omitting some of the books that the Catholics had included. Consequently, since the Bibles of the three major groupings do not contain all of the same writings, the term, Bible, means something technically different to each of them; and yet all believe that their officially approved books are sacred and complete. To avoid misunderstandings, we will refer explicitly to the Old and New Testaments in this book wherever practical. The term "Bible" will be used to mean the collected works.

The principal point of departure between Jews and Christians is over their understanding of the nature of the deity.

The Jewish conception of God is expressed perhaps most succinctly in the *Shema,* the prayer which is contained in Deuteronomy, the fifth book of the Old Testament:

> Hear, O Israel: The Lord is our God,
> the Lord is One. (Deuteronomy 6:4)

Although they accept the Hebrew Bible as their Old Testament, Christians include the New Testament, which deals with the life and works of Jesus of Nazareth. The Christian viewpoint is that Jesus was the Messiah, or Christ, and that He was the Son of God. Christians believe in the Trinity, the doctrine that the deity is composed of three coexistent principles, the Father, the Son, and the Holy Spirit (or Holy Ghost).

The Old Testament was written by many authors over thousands of years. The period it covers dates from before the Hebrew people had developed a written system of their own, but it is believed that the early books of the Old Testament were preserved from generation to generation by oral tradition. The last Old Testament book was written about 500 years before the birth of Jesus. The early Christians developed a calendar which measured historical time according to whether it preceded or followed the birth of Christ. Hence our designations of BC, for "Before Christ" (or "Before the Common Era": BCE, as Jews express it), and AD, Latin for *Anno Domini,* which means "Year of Our Lord."

Later we will deal with a serious mistake that was made when our present calendar was established. Not only was no zero position provided to separate BC from

AD, but the birth of Jesus was miscalculated by between four and seven years—figures which are based on comparisons of the Gospels with non-biblical data.

Not one of the original manuscripts of the Old or New Testament is known to exist. But believers hold that these texts were divinely-inspired documents and that they were kept accurate through the guidance of God and the extreme care of the scribes who copied and recopied the ancient scrolls during a period of nearly 5000 years.

But what about the reliability of these documents from an historical perspective? How do they compare with the evidence that derives from non-biblical sources?

Until about a century ago, some knowledgeable scholars scoffed at the idea that the Old Testament records actual historical events. Such scholars considered it to be basically a collection of myths, folk tales, and other legends, without factual substance. However, with the advent of archaeology, artifacts from many ancient cultures began to turn up which seemed to corroborate the biblical accounts.

Take, for instance, two biblical accounts which are generally well known today: the story of Noah and the Flood and the story of Joshua and the Battle of Jericho. We have selected these two stories for detailed examination, but there are many more which we will touch on later in this chapter.

Besides the one in the Old Testament book of Genesis, there are a number of accounts about the flood which seems to have inundated a substantial portion of the earth. Stories about this great deluge can be found in the legends of many cultures, from the ancient Egyptians to the aborigines of Australia, from the South American Fuegians to the Eskimos. In fact, almost every culture in every corner of the globe has a story about the same kind of totally-destructive waters which took all but a few lives—just as in the story of Noah.

While these stories of a great natural catastrophe

differ somewhat from culture to culture, four basic elements remain constant in the narratives.

According to Dr. Arthur C. Custance,[1] a student of cuneiform and Middle Eastern languages and a fellow of the Royal Canadian Anthropological Institute, the various cultural accounts relating to the flood share the following four motifs:

1. The catastrophe is a judgment on the people by an angry deity.

2. Only one man is warned of the flood. He is thus able to save not only himself, but also his family and his friends.

3. Except for these few survivors—the ancestors of the present population—everyone dies in the flood.

4. Animals and birds play a part either by being protected by the survivors or by giving them assistance in some way.

Dr. Custance notes that the extra-biblical accounts always record that the survivors landed on a local mountain. This includes Mount Parnassus in Greece and the Himalayas in India. In America, an Indian account has survivors land on Keddie Peak in California's Sacramento Valley.

The Hebrew account in the Bible has Noah and his family coming to rest on Mount Ararat in modern-day Turkey. There, at the 14,000-foot level, a boat-like structure has been reported by explorers and historians of several civilizations from as early as 700 BC. Spy planes and satellites have photographed the structure on Mount Ararat, and in 1955 an expedition filmed the recovery of wood from the structure nearly 35 feet below the ice surface.

In addition to these documented findings, geologists who have climbed Mount Everest have found sea shells. Other finds there include aquatic fossils, fish bones, clam shells, and the shells of sea snails.

As a result of these discoveries, there can be little doubt that there was once, indeed, a worldwide flood, as the Old Testament records. This doesn't mean, of course, that science can corroborate every detail of the story of Noah, but rather that the story is at least based on an actual event.

But what about the famous story in the book of Joshua, which tells how the Hebrews arrived in the Promised Land?

After the Hebrews left Egypt, they spent forty years in the wilderness until they came to the edge of what the Bible calls Canaan, a land named for the Canaanites and other ancient peoples who lived there. The refugees had to take the stronghold of Jericho if they were to penetrate the land they believed had been promised to them by God through their first patriarch, Abram, later called Abraham.

According to the biblical account, after the death of Moses, Joshua served as the general of the Hebrews, but it was God who gave the orders to take the stronghold. The tactics were very strange for a military operation.

The men of war under Joshua were to circle Jericho once daily for six days. They were to be accompanied by seven priests. Each of these carried a *shofar,* or ram's horn, which went before the Ark of the Covenant. This was the chest in which the two Tablets of the Law (the Ten Commandments) were kept. God had given the Ten Commandments to Moses on Mount Sinai years before, after the Hebrews had left Egypt.

On the seventh day of circling Jericho, the priests were to blow their trumpets and the people were to shout.

> The wall of the city will fall down flat, and the people will go up every man straight ahead. (Joshua 6:5)

That was God's promise to Joshua. The Bible records that the walls did fall and that Joshua's people swarmed straight ahead, taking Jericho and eventually reaching the Promised Land.

But did this really happen? Is there any evidence

outside the scriptural account to substantiate the Battle of Jericho?

Excavations begun at the site of Jericho in 1906 eventually proved that this walled city was one of the world's most ancient settlements, dating from as early as 7000 BC during the Neolithic Period. Archaeologists discovered that between the time the city was founded and the time that it was probably conquered by Joshua and the Hebrews—which appears to have occurred around 1300 BC—the walls of the city had fallen and been rebuilt many times. In some cases, the walls of Jericho may have been brought down by enemies laying siege to the city—but there is also another possibility to consider. Geologists, noting the great amount of seismic activity in the area, have suggested that the walls may have been vulnerable to frequent earthquakes.

We do not know, of course, whether or not it was an earthquake that brought down the walls when Joshua and the Hebrews besieged the city; but the idea is appealing since the biblical story tells us that the walls fell by themselves when the priests blew on the *shofar*. One thing, however, is certain, as far as modern science is concerned. Around 1300 BC, when the Hebrews were in the process of conquering the land of Canaan on their way to the Promised Land, the walls of Jericho *did* fall. Indeed, according to archaeologists involved in the excavations, the walls fell *outward*—which would have made it possible for the Hebrews to have entered the city, "every man straight ahead." Thus, all of the evidence would seem to confirm the historical basis of the story of Joshua and the Battle of Jericho—in the same way that the story of Noah and the Flood has been confirmed in other sources.

Perhaps the most important series of documents relating to the Old Testament to have been discovered in modern times is the *Dead Sea Scrolls*. Until 1947 when these remarkable documents were found in the Qumran Caves near the Dead Sea, the oldest-known copy of the Book of Isaiah was from about 900 AD. Paleographers checked a copy of Isaiah found in the

Dead Sea Scrolls and determined that it was written about 125 BC. Yet in spite of the more than one-thousand-year difference between the two manuscripts, it was found that there was only about a five percent deviation between their spelling, punctuation, and content. The scroll was almost identical to the present standard Hebrew Bible—after more than a thousand years.

The *Dead Sea Scrolls* have proven that over the course of some 4000 years, the words of the Old Testament were copied and handed down to us virtually unchanged. They testify to the verbal accuracy of the Old Testament, just as archaeological and historical findings testify to its historical reliability.

But what about the New Testament? How dependable a document is it?

Everyone who has seen a Christmas card is familiar with the Star of Bethlehem. But what was it? Since astronomy is so exact, astronomers have been able to suggest some scientific possibilities. Halley's Comet was visible in 11 BC, but this rules it out as a likely candidate for the Star of Bethlehem because the birth of Christ must have occurred a few years later. The suggestion has been made that the Star of Bethlehem was a supernova, but this is not considered likely. But a third possibility, which is now considered most likely to have been the case, is that there was a triple conjunction of the planets Jupiter, Saturn, and Venus. This planetary conjunction would have appeared as a star of extreme brightness, and would certainly have attracted the attention of astrologers—such as the wise men of the East who are mentioned in the Gospel of Saint Matthew may have been.

In 1925, the German scholar P. Schnabel deciphered a portion of a cuneiform tablet of Babylonian astrologers. Now, the Babylonians were such accurate students of the stars that they could predict—400 years before the birth of Christ—when eclipses would occur. And in this particular case, the wedge-shaped characters indicated that a triple conjunction of three planets had occurred in what would be 7 BC of our calendar, but which may well have been the year Christ was born.

What makes this so intriguing is that in the sixteenth century, the astronomer Johannes Kepler also observed the unusual conjunction of Saturn and Venus in the constellation of Pisces (the Fish). The significance of his discovery is the subject of greater examination later in this book.

The events recorded in the New Testament are corroborated by a number of independent accounts. The Jewish writer Josephus was born in Jerusalem shortly after the death of Jesus. Josephus deserted to the Romans during the siege of Jerusalem, so he is naturally considered a traitor by many Jews and his works are often criticized for their historical inaccuracies. However, though some scholars question the authenticity of his writings, what he had to say about Jesus is extremely interesting.

The Gospels mention that Jesus was tried before Annas and Caiaphas, who are described as being the high priests of the Jews. Yet, by Jewish custom, there could only have been one high priest at a given time. Josephus explains that Annas was the former high priest while his son-in-law, Caiaphas, was high priest when Pontius Pilate governed Judea. The Jews considered that high priests held the office for life. Josephus also tells us that Caiaphas' first name was Joseph.

The Gospels report that John the Baptist criticized the tetrarch Herod Antipas for his illegal marriage to Herodias, his brother's wife. So to punish John, Herodias had her daughter by her first husband dance before Herod, the girl's stepfather. Herod was so well pleased that he offered the girl anything she wanted. At her mother's coaching, she demanded the head of John the Baptist.

Josephus, while giving a different motivation than the Gospels for John's beheading, provides two elements they omit. He mentions that the teenaged daughter was named Salome and that John was imprisoned at the Fortress of Macherus.

There are countless other fascinating pieces of information recorded by Josephus in complete independence of the Gospels. Later we will look at Josephus' account in more detail and we will also examine what some of the Roman writers who lived at the time of Jesus had to say about him.

In this chapter, we have offered a number of examples to prove what the experts confirm again and again: that the Bible is an extraordinarily accurate work with a basis in historical fact. With the dependability of the Bible established, let us now turn to some of its ancient prophecies which are clues in our search for the historic Jesus.

3

MESSIANIC PROPHECIES
AND THE STORY OF
THE NATIVITY

The New Testament repeatedly refers to the acts of Jesus as fulfilling Old Testament prophecies. While Jews and Christians may disagree as to whether Jesus was indeed the Messiah, the fact remains that those who wrote the Gospels were consciously building upon the ancient prophecies of the Old Testament.

It is our purpose in searching for the historic Jesus to study the whole story as found in both the Old and New Testaments. We will examine all the evidence, hear all the witnesses, and sift through everything for answers and clues to help us in our quest.

To do that, we must start with the Old Testament promises about the coming Messiah. Then we will examine New Testament claims as to how those prophecies were fulfilled. In the process, we will have taken a necessary step in our search for the historic Jesus.

Because of the nature of ancient Hebrew culture —in which religion was so completely intertwined with legal and political matters—the Old Testament sometimes refers to the coming of the Messiah in religious terms, sometimes in political terms, and sometimes in both at once. Thus, the Messiah might assume the form of prophet, priest, or king—or he might combine all of these roles. It was an ancient Hebrew custom to set priests and kings apart from the general population by anointing them with oil.

But before we examine those prophecies of the Old Testament which are specifically concerned with a Messiah—that is, with a figure who will *deliver* the children of Israel from their suffering at the hands of alien peoples—we must first establish their context by examining some of the promises that God made to the great Hebrew patriarchs. For if Jesus is interpreted as fulfilling the Scriptures, as the New Testament claims, then he can also be viewed as representing a continuation of the patriarchs and prophets of the Old Testament. It should be clear, of course, that while these matters hinge on personal beliefs, our concern is the manner in which the New Testament builds upon the Old Testament.

The first Old Testament prophecy is the promise God made to Abraham that he would be the ancestor of a great people, and that this people would be given a land of their own—a land which has variously been called Canaan, Israel, Judea, Palestine, and, since 1948, the State of Israel.

Abraham had been born in Ur, a most ancient city of what is known as the "fertile crescent" in Mesopotamia. The Chaldeans who lived in Ur had a religion which involved such practices as moon worship. Abraham, however, (who was known as Abram at first) was summoned by God to leave his homeland and to go to a land which God would show him.

Abraham and his wife, Sarah, journeyed northwest around the great Sahara Desert and eventually worked their way down, inland from the Mediterranean Sea, toward Egypt. His nomadic life took Abraham into Egypt and back into the land then called Canaan, named for one of the pagan peoples who lived there.

The first Hebrew patriarch had neither a son nor

an inch of ground when God appeared to him in the
land of Canaan:

> Now lift up your eyes and look from the
> place where you are, northward and south-
> ward and eastward and westward; for all the
> land which you see I will give to you and to
> your descendants forever. (Genesis 13:14–
> 15)

God's promise was partially fulfilled when Abraham and Sarah had a son, Isaac. His sons, in turn, included Jacob, who was later called Israel. Israel had
twelve sons who became the Twelve Tribes of Israel.
One of these sons was called Judah.

The second part of God's promise to Abraham
had not been fulfilled centuries later when the Hebrews
left Egyptian bondage and set out for the Promised
Land. At Mount Sinai, when Moses received the Ten
Commandments, God made him this promise:

> I will raise up a prophet from among
> their countrymen like you. (Deuteronomy
> 18:18)

Moses' successor, Joshua, captured Jericho and led
the twelve tribes into Canaan where they eventually
possessed the land promised to their ancestor, Abraham.
David was next in the line of major prophetic
figures. The shepherd boy who grew up to be king over
all of the twelve tribes also received a promise from
God:

> When your days are complete and you
> lie down with your fathers, I will raise up
> from your descendants after you one who will
> come forth from you, and I will establish his
> kingdom. He shall build a house for My name,
> and I will establish the throne of his kingdom
> forever. (II Sam. 7:12–13; I Chron. 17:11)

David's son was Solomon, whom the Old Testament refers to as the wisest man who ever lived. Solomon built the First Temple. However, David's grandson engaged in a civil war which split the monarchy. A few hundred years later, in 722 BC, the Assyrians carried off the ten northern tribes, who vanished into oblivion.

In 586 BC, Nebuchadnezzar led the Babylonians against Jerusalem. The two remaining tribes were deported to the area where their ancestor, Abraham, had been born.

The Persians, who succeeded the Babylonians, were less inclined to persecute the Hebrews, because they shared with them a belief in monotheism. Therefore, the Persian king, Cyrus, gave some of the Hebrews permission to return to Jerusalem. Those who did return were henceforward called "Jews," after the fourth of Jacob's twelve sons, Judah.

Over the centuries, the people had suffered from a civil war, exile, and other political and military disasters. And even when they had finally returned to their homeland, their troubles weren't over, for still other military occupations followed.

They were conquered by the Macedonians under Alexander the Great; and after Alexander, the Ptolemies of Egypt and the Seleucids of Syria continued the occupation. The Jews enjoyed a brief period of home rule under the Maccabees and their descendants who overthrew the Greek-speaking Seleucids. But the Romans under Pompey took Jerusalem in 63 BC and ruled from Rome through such local monarchs as the merciless King Herod of Idumean-Arabian descent.

That was the situation when the Gospel writers, Matthew and Luke, opened their account of Jesus' birth. Both Matthew and Luke trace Jesus' genealogy through Joseph, Jesus' earthly parent, back to David and Abraham.

By the time Jesus was born, messianic expectations were high. The Jews suffering under the Roman occupation could study the Scriptures for prophecies relating directly to the coming of the Messiah. Among the attributes of the Messiah specified by the prophets, the following are the most significant:

1. The Messiah would come from the line of King David, in fulfillment of God's promise.

2. The Messiah would be born of a virgin. One of the most popular messianic prophets, Isaiah, had written in about 735 BC: "Therefore, the Lord Himself will give you a sign: Behold, a virgin shall be with child and bear a son, and she will call his name Emmanuel." (Isaiah 7:14)

3. The Messiah would live awhile in Egypt. According to Hosea, a minor prophet who lived around 750 BC, or before the ten northern tribes of Israel had been exiled by the Assyrians, God had said: "Out of Egypt have I called My son." (Hos. 11:1)

It was expected that someone would come ahead of the Messiah and prepare the way for him. This was based on the prophecies of another minor prophet, Malachi. Malachi is not really a proper name. The word means "my messenger," and nothing is really known about the author personally, though it is calculated that he wrote at about 460 BC. Malachi had written:

> Behold, I am going to send you Elijah the prophet before the coming of the great and terrible day of the Lord, and he will restore the hearts of the fathers to their children, and the hearts of the children to their fathers. (Malachi 4:5, 6)

But Isaiah is the prophet most clearly associated with the promise of the coming of the Messiah:

> For a child will be born to us. And the government will rest upon His shoulders. And His name shall be called . . . Prince of Peace. (Isaiah 9:6)

Prince of Peace! What a hope for people who had suffered so much through the ages. They were ready for a deliverer!

The following recreation of scenes from the Gospels presents the historical characters in episodes that have been enriched by research from some of the non-scriptural sources that have already been mentioned.

In the Gospel of Saint Matthew, we are introduced to persons not included in the Gospel of Saint Luke—perhaps because Matthew was writing for a different audience and purpose than the Gentile chronicler.

A number of wise men, or magi, arrived in Jerusalem from the east, probably from the Mesopotamian area beyond the Sahara Desert. They had a question:

"Where is he that is born King of the Jews? For we saw his star in the east, and have come to worship him." (Matthew 2:2)

Eventually, of course, word of this reached the power-mad monarch who had killed his own sons and wife to keep his throne. Herod gathered his chief priests and scribes together in the palace. The former were members of a powerful group that had great authority over the spiritual lives of the Jews. The scribes were prestigious laymen who worked with the priesthood and even had seats in the high council at Jerusalem, the Great Sanhedrin. The scribes were masters of the Scriptures who were often men of independent means.

Herod looked over these members of the religious elite and demanded: "Where is the Christ to be born?" (Matthew 2:4)

The priests and scribes exchanged uneasy glances. Herod's merciless attitude was well known. His body showed the ravages of his advancing years and tensions. Once he had been an extremely handsome man who could match any warrior in the field with spear and bow. But now, nearing the age of 70, he had become flabby and dissipated. His iron will and brutal determination remained unchanged, however, and so the religious leaders answered Herod immediately: "In Bethlehem of Judea."

"How do you know that?" Herod demanded.

"It has been written by the prophet . . ."

"Which prophet?"

"Micah, a country dweller who was somewhat younger but lived about the same time as Isaiah, and before Jeremiah."

The king nodded. "Micah then lived about 700 years ago. What did he say about the Messiah and Bethlehem?"

One of the priests glanced uneasily at his companions and quoted from memory. "And you, Bethlehem, land of Judah, are by no means least among the leaders of Judah; for out of you shall come forth a ruler, who will shepherd My people of Israel." (Micah 5:2; Matthew 2:6)

Herod dismissed the Jews and secretly called in the magi. He gazed thoughtfully at their foreign garments, which bore the signs of a thousand-mile journey. The king's eyes narrowed thoughtfully. These men had not come that distance without strong convictions that the star they had followed meant something unique. They believed that the King of the Jews had been born. But they were wise men; Herod would have to be shrewd in phrasing his questions.

"What time does the star appear?" he asked. (Matthew 2:7)

It was a curious question, for the star hovered over Bethlehem, a mere five miles away. When he had heard their answer, Herod smiled—as if to indicate humble acceptance. "Go," he said, "and make careful search for the child. And when you have found him, report to me, that I too may come and worship him." (Matthew 2:8)

The wise men bowed deeply and left the king's palace. Herod pursed his thick lips in anticipation. He had plotted well, and soon he would find and remove the threat to his throne.

The wise men found the infant Jesus with his mother in a house and presented him with gifts, as the Gospel of Saint Matthew declares.

The Gospel of Saint Luke mentions neither the wise men, Herod, nor the house. Instead, the Greek physician who is credited with writing both the Gospel that bears his name and the Book of Acts, which follows the Gospels, stresses other aspects of the nativity story.

Luke tells us that the time for Mary to be delivered of her first-born approached while she and Joseph were in Bethlehem. They had come there to register for a Roman census, since Joseph was of the house and lineage of David. At the time, the couple was betrothed but not yet married. Traditionally, from earliest times, there was a two-part arrangement to a Jewish marriage. The betrothal was as binding as a marriage contract, and it even required a bill of divorcement if the engagement were broken. However, a marriage was not considered official until it had been consummated. And although Mary was pregnant, Joseph and Mary had had no sexual relations.

An angel had explained to them that it was the Holy Spirit that had implanted her virgin womb.

Luke has given his nativity scene a wealth of concrete detail. He tells us that the little town was so crowded that there was no room for the expectant Mary. Joseph and Mary found room in a stable, where the infant Jesus was born and wrapped in swaddling clothes. Outside, as shepherds watched their flocks, an angel appeared to announce the news of the birth:

> Do not be afraid; for behold, I bring you good news of great joy which shall be for all the people; for today in the city of David there has been born for you a Savior, who is Christ the Lord. (Luke 2:10)

Luke tells us that the shepherds came and saw the baby and then told abroad all that they had seen and heard.

But the Gospel of Saint Luke doesn't mention the horrors which Matthew records as being the aftermath of Herod's wrath.

*   *   *

The magi had departed to their own country without reporting back to Herod about where they had found the child born to be King of the Jews. When he found out that he had been deceived, Herod was furious. He called in the Roman officers assigned to his garrison and screamed at them: "I want every male Jew, aged two or under, killed immediately."

The centurion, holding his plumed helmet respectfully against his chest, shot a quick glance at the raving king and then turned to the seasoned veterans of many campaigns who stood impassively beside him.

It was clear from Herod's expression that the orders were firm. The centurion saluted and, followed by his attendant officers, went out to do the king's bidding.

During the nights that followed, Roman soldiers with torchlights would break into Jewish homes and either seize or instantly kill the baby boys that they found. In the ensuing days, as frantic parents tried to hide their sons or slip them out of the little town, the short Roman swords slashed into small bodies.

The wailing of the bereaved women could be heard all over Bethlehem and for miles around. As it had been prophesied, Rachel wept for her children and could not be comforted.

Herod, patting his fat paunch, was satisfied. "They're all dead," he told himself with pride. "The throne is safe! Nobody can take it from me now."

But Herod was wrong.

Joseph had obeyed God's command to take Mary and the infant Jesus and flee to Egypt. Thus, while the women of Bethlehem shrieked in their grief, Jesus was safe in the land of the Pharaohs. There he would remain until God called him out again.

Such is the story of the nativity, as told by the Gospels of Matthew and Luke. Millions of people know the story and annually celebrate the birth of Jesus with the pageantry of Christmas. But what about the historical basis of the two Gospel accounts? Can they be supported by documents and records from the period?

The chronicler Josephus, whom we have cited previously, wrote extensively about Herod. Born Yoseph ben Mattityahu ha-Cohen about 38 AD, Josephus was a Palestinian Jew of a priestly family who became a politician and a soldier, but is best known for his historian's role. Josephus apparently drew much of his material about Herod from Nicholas of Damascus, a Greek adviser and confidant of the king. Josephus obviously didn't like Herod, but nevertheless provided the world with a good deal of knowledge about one of the most infamous figures of history.

If Josephus is correct, Herod was born around 73 BC, the grandson of an Idumean who had converted to Judaism. An astute politician who knew how to gain the trust of the Romans, Herod rose from governor of Galilee to tetrarch, finally becoming king in 37 BC.

Josephus dwells at length on Herod's despotic rule and includes detailed accounts of his thousands of murders. Yet the Jewish historian says not a word about the horrible event which has come to be known as the Massacre of the Innocents. There is no doubt Herod would have been capable of carrying out such a massacre. But the question arises why, if it actually occurred, it was not recorded by Josephus.

Luke alone mentions the Roman census, and in so precise a manner as to indicate some firsthand knowledge of it.

He also mentions that the birth of Jesus took place during the reign of the emperor Augustus, when Quirinius was governor of Syria. Historical records show that Quirinius was governor of Syria in 6 AD—but there is no evidence to support that he held this office at about 6 BC when Jesus was born.

The other points mentioned by Luke are correct. Augustus ruled from 63 BC until his death in 14 AD. The Romans took censuses to determine the taxation of occupied nations. Palestine was under the governor of Syria at the time of Augustus' rule, with Herod serving as king in Judea. Later, procurators took over in the south while Herod's son, Herod Antipas, reigned as tetrarch in the northern province of Galilee.

Basically, the Gospel nativity stories are corroborated by history—with some exceptions, such as the Massacre of the Innocents.

The Star of Bethlehem is another check point. Since astronomers can today calculate the location of heavenly bodies at any time in the past or future, based on their precise patterns of travel through the universe, they can also discern whether there was any unusual heavenly light around the time of Jesus' birth, as recounted by Matthew.

While several explanations have been offered to account for the Star of Bethlehem—including that it was a comet—the famed astronomer, Johannes Kepler, offered the most plausible answer. On December 17, 1603, Kepler was in Prague looking through a telescope at the night sky. Suddenly Kepler saw the conjunction of two planets on the same degree of longitude. The two planets, Saturn and Jupiter—from the constellation of Pisces—gave the appearance of being a single bright star. Impressed by what he had seen, Kepler remembered that Jewish astrologers had predicted that the Messiah would come when there was a conjunction of Jupiter and Saturn in the constellation of Pisces.

Following his insight, Kepler performed some calculations and came up with the startling discovery that, indeed, on December 4, in 7 BC, a conjunction of Jupiter and Saturn in the constellation of Pisces had occurred. The two heavenly bodies had actually met twice earlier that year, on May 29 and October 3. Of course, these were really only close encounters in the sense that they appeared to be merging in the vast reaches of space. On the third conjunction, however, the two planets met on the same longitudinal degree.

Kepler's theory was given wide acclaim for a while, but then was rejected and forgotten. His hypothesis was regarded as inadequate even as late as the 19th century. In 1925, however, a fascinating new piece of evidence was uncovered which brought Kepler's theory back into prominence.

As we noted in the previous chapter, P. Schnabel, a German scholar working with neo-Babylonian cuneiform (wedge-shaped characters used in writing by such ancient peoples as the Assyrians and Babylonians), discovered that the astrology school at Sippar, Babylonia, had carefully recorded the conjunction of Jupiter and Saturn in the constellation of Pisces—in what would have been 7 BC according to modern calendars.

Kepler had been vindicated centuries after his discovery of what had caused the visual phenomenon of the Star of Bethlehem.

There are two questions posed by Kepler's discovery with respect to the ancient Babylonian records. What about the two earlier conjunctions of those same planets in May and October? Why has Jesus' birth been located seven years after it occurred?

The Gospel of Saint Matthew records that the magi came to Jerusalem from the east. A glance at a map of the Middle East shows that east of Jerusalem there is a vast desert. It would have taken such travelers a long time to follow the caravan trails from their probable starting point in Mesopotamia—present-day Iran or Iraq. Could the earlier conjunctions have prompted the magi to begin their months-long trek to see the one who would be born "King of the Jews"? Their calculations could have made them aware that the conjunction would happen again in early December.

It is speculation to locate Jesus' birth in 7 BC, but it is a well-known fact that the monk who set up our present calendar made a serious error.

Denys le Petit proposed in 532 AD that the calendar be based on the Christian Era. His calculations located the birth of Jesus on December 25 of the Roman year 753. The Church later set Jesus' birth several years earlier than Denys' calculations. The Christian Era was later set to coincide with Saturday, January 1.

Another problem was the omission of a zero position between the years 1 BC and 1 AD. The net result of the confusion is that Jesus' birth is now variously placed by knowledgeable scholars at 4, 5, 6, or 7 BC—with some researchers favoring an even earlier date.

The reliability of the Gospel account is again proven by the fact that Herod's death has been fixed at April 4, 4 BC. Since Matthew tells us that Herod was alive at the time of Jesus' birth, the birth itself must have been prior to April 4, 4 BC. But just how much before?

In Luke's account of the nativity, Jesus is born during the census that Caesar Augustus imposed on Judea when Quirinius was governor of Syria. Roman records prove that Augustus died in 14 AD—a fact which coincides with the scriptural account. However, such records indicate that while Quirinius was governor of Syria, he was not governor at the time indicated in Luke's narrative. This immediately poses the question as to why the Gospel conflicts with historical records.

Publius Sulpicius Quirinius (or Cyrenius) was a Roman governor who died in 21 AD. His service includes a period during which he was consul at Rome in 12 BC. He is also known to have subdued the Homanadenses in Galatia somewhat later. He was sent as Roman governor to Syria in 6 AD for the specific purpose of assessing taxes, which meant taking a census of the people.

Thus, if the historical records are correct, Quirinius' census would have occurred about a dozen years too late to coincide with the nativity. However, Luke has added a statement which might someday resolve the discrepancy: "This was the first census taken while Quirinius was governor of Syria." (Luke 2:2)

First census? Could the census known to have been taken in 6 AD be a second one? Many such discrepancies have been satisfactorily resolved by later historical evidence, and perhaps it may turn out that Luke was correct after all.

For after nearly 2,000 years Luke's testimony is still highly regarded. As F. F. Bruce declared, "Where Luke has been suspected of inaccuracy, and accuracy has been vindicated by some inscriptural evidence, it may be legitimate to say that archaeology has confirmed the New Testament record."[1]

The mention of Archelaus in Matthew's nativity account offers a final clue about the accuracy of his Gospel. Matthew tells us that when Joseph heard that King Herod was dead, he returned to the land of Israel with Mary and the young Jesus. Christians therefore claim that Hosea's prophecy that the Messiah would be called out of Egypt had been fulfilled. But Matthew adds that when Joseph had heard that Archelaus was reigning in place of his father Herod, he was afraid to return to Judea.

Who, then, was Archelaus?

His father was the infamous King Herod and his mother was a Samaritan. Archelaus was born about 22 BC, so he was around eighteen when he inherited his father's throne. Although his right to the throne was subject to confirmation by the emperor in Rome, Archelaus proceeded to demonstrate his authority to the Jews in his domain.

He sent soldiers out to kill 3,000 people in an attempt to prevent a riot at the Passover which came soon after Herod's death. But while Archelaus was on his way to Rome to seek confirmation of his right to the throne, an insurrection began in Judea. Quintilius Varus, president of Syria, acted in Archelaus' absence to quell a Jewish uprising which began at Pentecost (50 days after Passover) and raged for a few months. Therefore, when Archelaus returned from Rome, frustrated because Augustus had made him an ethnarch instead of a king like his father, he took his anger out on the Jews by persecuting them even more harshly. From historical records we know that Archelaus was deposed in 6 AD, so Jesus' return from Egypt must have occurred before that year.

Matthew concludes his account of the nativity by saying that Archelaus' presence in Judea caused Joseph to go on to Galilee and live in the town of Nazareth, thus fulfilling another Old Testament prophecy.

Luke, on the other hand, recounts an incident in

which the infant Jesus is presented to the temple elders, but then passes over the rest of this period by saying only that the family went to Galilee "to their own city of Nazareth." (Luke 2:39) Luke thus confirms Matthew on this point.

It is strange that the Scriptures are totally silent on the subject of Jesus' boyhood in the town of Nazareth. This is a mystery which we shall examine.

4

THE MYSTERY OF
WHERE JESUS SPENT
HIS BOYHOOD

Anyone reading the Gospels would logically think that Jesus grew up in Nazareth. But the only two records in the New Testament aren't that exact, and so legends have persisted that Jesus' boyhood also included trips to Britain, India, and other far-away countries. We'll examine those in Chapter 5.

In order to present a balanced perspective on the question of where Jesus grew up, we must consider all possibilities.

Matthew, whose book is placed first in the New Testament, says that Joseph, having returned from Egypt after Herod's death, was afraid to stay in Archelaus' territory. Therefore "he departed for the regions of Galilee, and came and resided in a city called Nazareth, that what was spoken through the prophets might be fulfilled, 'He shall be called a Nazarene.'" (Matt. 2:22, 23)

The next time Matthew mentions Jesus, he is some eighteen years older and about to begin his public ministry by coming to John the Baptist at the Jordan River.

Incidentally, there is no Old Testament passage that corresponds to the prophecy Matthew cites. In fact, the town of Nazareth isn't mentioned at all in the Old Testament. But there are various references in the New Testament to texts which must once have been included in the Scriptures, but have been either lost or abandoned.

Luke gives two pieces of information about Jesus' boyhood. This third Gospel reports that after Joseph and Mary had performed everything according to the Law of the Lord, they returned to Galilee, to their own city of Nazareth.

> And the Child continued to grow and become strong, increasing in wisdom, and the grace of God was upon him. (Luke 2:39–40)

Luke then recounts an incident from when Jesus was twelve, which is the only story about Jesus' boyhood in the Gospels. In a moment, we will recreate that episode, but first it is important to understand why one Gospel may have a story about Jesus which is omitted in one or more of the others. Such is the case with the story from Jesus' boyhood which only Luke recounts.

Each of the Gospel writers penned his material for a specific purpose, and for a particular audience. None intended to tell everything about Jesus, as a modern biographer might. Rather, each of the four emphasized different aspects of Jesus' life.

Some scholars claim that the Gospel of Saint Mark was written first, although Matthew is placed first in the New Testament. The author, writing somewhere between 64 and 85 AD, wrote in Greek for Greek-speaking Christians. His Gospel is considered the basis for Matthew and Luke, the two other Synoptic Gospels, and was helpful to John's narrative.

The Gospel of Saint Matthew, probably written between 75 and 95 AD, was for Jews who had become Christians. Matthew intended to prove that Jesus was the Messiah the Jews had been expecting.

The Gospel of Saint Luke is generally located at about 75 AD, or soon thereafter. Luke aimed to reach Gentile or non-Jewish readers, and his purpose was to present the facts to a particular Roman official and other readers outside of Judea. Luke hoped to allay some of the suspicions which had arisen about the new sect.

The Gospel of Saint John is usually placed between 95 and 105 AD. In contrast to the three Synoptic Gospels, whose emphasis is historical, John emphasizes the mystical dimension. John was interested in solidifying his readers' faith, and chose the stories he recounts accordingly.

It is John's mention of three Passovers that indicates that Jesus' public ministry lasted about three and a half years. And it is in John that names and events omitted in the three Synoptic Gospels can be found.

There is controversy over who really wrote each of the four Gospels, but there is no doubt that each author included the stories which were pertinent to his point of view.

Luke's narrative was originally joined to the Acts of the Apostles, which is now a separate book in the New Testament. Luke wanted his readers to understand the events that shaped Christianity, including how Jesus passed his early life. Therefore, Luke chose to recount an incident from Jesus' boyhood which took place in Jerusalem.

It was required for all able-bodied male Jews to attend the Passover in Jerusalem. Mary, mother of Jesus, accompanied her husband on this annual pilgrimage. Jesus didn't make the trip until he was twelve, which was the age when a Jewish boy came of age.

The Passover, commemorating the exodus of the Jews from Egypt, was on the fourteenth day of the first month of the sacred year, called Nisan. This coincided with either March or April, depending on the full moon required for the observance. It was at a Passover feast that Jesus, when he was about 33 years old, predicted the events that were to bring him to the cross and change the lives of countless millions over the next two millennia.

As a boy of twelve, Jesus would have been well

versed in the story of the original Passover. It was written in the sacred book called the *Torah,* a Hebrew word meaning "teaching" or "law." In a restricted sense, the *Torah* was composed of the five books of Moses, called the *Pentateuch.*

Moses had repeatedly tried to get Pharaoh to free the Hebrews who had been slaves in Egypt. A series of plagues visited by God upon the ruler didn't soften his heart. Finally, God told Moses that He would slay all first-born Egyptian sons:

> I will go through the land of Egypt on that night, and will strike down the first-born in the land of Egypt, both man and beast; and against all the gods of Egypt I will execute judgment—I am the Lord.
> And the blood shall be a sign for you on the houses where you live; and when I see the blood I will pass over you, and no plague will befall you to destroy you when I strike the land of Egypt. (Ex. 12:12–13)

The Pharaoh's stricken people bewailed their losses that midnight "from the first-born of Pharaoh who sat on his throne to the first-born of the captive who was in the dungeon, and all the first-born of cattle." (Ex. 12:29)

The Hebrews under Moses were hastily ejected from Egypt. They began their long trek to the Promised Land, passing Mount Sinai along the way, where Moses received the Ten Commandments.

The descendants of the original Hebrew slaves never forgot their Egyptian bondage, for God had clearly specified that the story be handed down from generation to generation. God told Moses:

> And you shall observe this event as an ordinance for you and your children forever.
> And it will come about when you enter the land which the Lord will give you, as He has promised, that you shall observe this rite.
> And it will come about when your chil-

dren will say to you, "What does this rite mean to you?" that you shall say, "It is a Passover sacrifice to the Lord who passed over the houses of the sons of Israel in Egypt when He smote the Egyptians, but spared our homes." (Ex. 12:24–27)

During the first Passover that Jesus spent in Jerusalem, he might conceivably have encountered two men who would play important roles in his later career, Joseph of Arimathea and Nicodemus, though in Luke's account they are not mentioned by name. Luke tells us that Joseph and Mary, returning to Galilee after the Jerusalem observances, had gone a day's journey before they realized that Jesus was not in the caravan among their relatives and acquaintances. So they returned to the city, where they found Jesus sitting in the temple courtyard with the teachers, listening and asking questions. What follows is a recreation of Luke's account.

Joseph of Arimathea seemed amused. "So," he said with a faint smile, "you have made up your mind to be a rabbi, have you?"

The boy answered, "Yes, Master."

Joseph stroked his beard. He was a member of the Jewish high council, the Sanhedrin. He was a rich man, and considered good, who had a strong inclination toward the things of God. "Are you prepared to learn, my boy?" he continued his questioning. "Are you prepared to spend many years with your head buried in studies and prayer?"

He reached out and gently touched Jesus' smooth chin. "Are you prepared to do that until the day you lift up your bearded chin and become one of us?"

Joseph smiled at Nicodemus, one of the other learned men who were watching the exchange. Nicodemus was a Pharisee, the foremost Jewish sect, and also a member of the Sanhedrin.

"If God be willing," said Jesus.

Joseph, thinking of what had been going on for the past several hours, said to Jesus: "You have asked profound questions far beyond one of your years. Tell me, what kind of teacher would you be?"

The boy frowned slightly. "What kind?"

Joseph explained: "The sages say there are those who teach with arrogance; those who teach that we must do our duty to God; those who teach we must obey him out of fear . . ."

Jesus interrupted. "I know what kind of teacher I want to be, Master."

Joseph and Nicodemus exchanged glances. "Tell us, my boy," *he said.*

Jesus answered: "You know the story the great Hillel himself has told?" *Hillel was a rabbi who had been born in Babylonia and had come to Jerusalem to study when he was 40 years old. He founded the Bet Hillel (House of Hillel), an academy where he taught. King Herod had appointed Hillel president of the Sanhedrin, where he had served until his death in 10 AD. If Jesus was born in 7 BC, Hillel would still have been alive when Jesus was 12 years old.*

Since the famous scholar was known for two sayings, Joseph pursed his lips and asked Jesus, "Which story?"

"The one about the man who went to Rabbi Hillel and asked him to tell him the whole of Judaism while the man stood on one foot."

Joseph smiled in recollection, urging the boy to finish the story.

"Rabbi Hillel told the man, 'Don't do to your neighbor what you wouldn't want done to you. This is the whole Law. The rest is commentary.' "

Joseph laughed. "He thinks like a bearded one already!"

At this point, Jesus' parents, Mary and Joseph, arrived upon the scene. They were as astonished as the elders at their son's brilliance, but they were also parents who had spent three fruitless days looking for Jesus.

Mary cried, "Son, why have you treated us this

way? We've been anxiously looking for you!" (Luke 2:48)

The boy looked up into his mother's face and asked: "Why were you looking for me? Didn't you know that I had to be about my Father's business?" (Luke 2:49)

As Joseph and Mary walked away with Jesus, Joseph of Arimathea turned to Nicodemus and frowned. Then the rich merchant repeated wonderingly: "I had to be about my Father's business."

Luke closes his account of Jesus' infancy and boyhood with the incident in the temple, adding that his parents did not understand the statement he had made. But the boy returned to Nazareth with them and "continued in subjection to them; and his mother treasured all these things in her heart."

It was an important event, for it clearly showed Jesus had an early sense of mission. He had come for a purpose and already knew he had to be doing the work he had been sent to do. However, the story raises some important questions and offers some clues which may help in our search for the historical Jesus.

How could his parents, for example, have failed to miss their son for a whole day?

The most likely answer is that they assumed Jesus was with friends or relatives in the caravan heading from Jerusalem to Nazareth. As responsible parents, chosen by God for the unique ministry of rearing God's own Son (as the New Testament indicates), Joseph and Mary would not likely have let the boy out of their sight if they were not sure he was in other good hands.

But whose hands?

The Gospel writers tell us little about Joseph's family, except to say that he was of the line of David. Luke and Matthew disagree on Joseph's father's name. Matthew lists it as Jacob; Luke gives it as Eli or Heli.

Mary, wife of Joseph and mother of Jesus, had at least one sister and a near relative, Elizabeth. The sister's name is not given. But Elizabeth and her husband, the priest Zachariah, had a son in their old age. He became John the Baptist and was a relative of Jesus. Some researchers believe John and Jesus were second cousins, but this is not clear. In the New Testament, there are a number of people whose associations with Jesus are shrouded in mystery. For example, there is a perplexing lack of information about Joseph of Arimathea and, to a somewhat lesser extent, about Nicodemus.

Matthew introduces Joseph of Arimathea only after Jesus' death on the cross, but clearly indicates they had met before. The three other Gospels also mention the council member and briefly summarize his life only after the Crucifixion.

As a result, Joseph of Arimathea is the subject of a number of legends which have been handed down through the ages. For example, there is the legend that Jesus was the nephew of Joseph of Arimathea. Joseph is also said to have been a tin merchant, which is interesting in view of the fact that at the time the principal source of this product was Britain. If Joseph of Arimathea was Jesus' uncle, then he was the brother of either Joseph or Mary, Jesus' parents. However, it's unlikely two brothers would have been named Joseph, so the stronger possibility is that Mary, mother of Jesus, was the sister of Joseph of Arimathea.

These legends about Joseph of Arimathea have partly developed because of the New Testament's unusual way of dealing with him.

No modern story teller would logically expect to publish a narrative in which a vital character is not introduced early in the proceedings. Joseph of Arimathea was only important to the Gospel writers in one episode, and they felt no compunction to present him earlier.

But if Joseph of Arimathea was Jesus' uncle, it is logical that Jesus could have been traveling with him without worrying his parents. And Luke declares they had "relatives and acquaintances."

5

THE EIGHTEEN
MISSING YEARS
IN JESUS' LIFE

Since the Gospels are silent on where Jesus was between the ages of twelve and thirty, we must look at other sources. There are many legends which seek to explain how Jesus spent the years before his public ministry began.

It is understood that these sources are not considered to be sacred, as believers hold the Bible to be. But in the same way that Jews, Catholics, and Protestants do not agree on which books should be in their respective Scriptures, or even the order of those books, so we must conclude that non-canonical material about Jesus should be examined for what it is.

A number of these apocryphal stories deal with questions which many people want answered about Jesus' young life. Here are a few examples:

1. Granting that Jesus had one of the greatest minds of all time, how did he learn so much about everything if he never left the little town of Nazareth? Isn't it possible he studied under the great teachers of other cultures? For example, Buddhism and Hinduism were already ancient religions before Jesus was born. So was Zoroastrianism. Couldn't Jesus have visited

some of the countries where these religions are followed, and learned from these faiths?

2. The resurrection of the dead and some of the other doctrines Jesus preached aren't exclusive to the Christian religion. Might Jesus have visited some place where such things were taught, like Egypt?

3. Since the Jews didn't even have a word for "bachelor," and thought every young man should marry, how come Jesus wasn't married? Wasn't there ever any romance in his life?

4. Could Jesus have been known under other names in some foreign countries, in the same way that even today his name is spelled and pronounced differently from country to country?

The answers to such questions cannot be given now, some twenty centuries after Jesus' life was recorded in the Gospels. We can only piece together hypotheses which are based on speculation, legends, and purported records of antiquity and claimed revelation.

Let's consider how certain unsubstantiated sources present Jesus' younger years.

According to the *Aquarian Gospels,* which list their source as "Levi's Akashic records," when Jesus was about twelve he left his homeland and journeyed to the far east. His travels took him to Persia (modern-day Iran) where he is said to have visited the magi who had followed the Star of Bethlehem. This reunion of the wise men and Jesus resulted in the transfiguration of all four, enveloping them in a blinding white light.

Jesus the boy is also said to have traveled on to the country of Tibet. This is an area now occupying about half a million square miles in southern Asia; it is southwest of China, northeast of India, and northwest of Burma.

There, the story goes, Jesus clashed with the lamas, or Buddhist monks. Jesus is said to have objected to some of their doctrines which conflicted with the lamas' concepts of doctrines they based on the teachings of Gautama Buddha, the Indian sage who founded Buddhism sometime around 500 BC.

The legend claims that the monks thrust Jesus outside the city wall where it was expected wild animals would devour him in the night. But travelers venturing forth the next morning were astonished to see that Jesus had not only not been eaten by the beasts, but had made friends with a tiger.

Another source suggests that Jesus may have been known as Isa and regarded as a prophet in the Kashmir-Tibet border area. In *Jesus Died in Kashmir,* the author, A. Faber-Kaiser, claims that a Russian explorer, Nicolai Notovich, who was reputedly traveling near the Kashmir-Tibet border around the end of the 19th century, came across data which shows that the fourteen-year-old Jesus was known as Isa, and that he studied several years among the Brahmins.

Brahmins were priests in the Hindu religion, which believes in a god named Brahma who created the universe. Most people in India accept this faith, which involves the separation of society into four major hereditary classes. Until recently the castes did not mix.

Consequently, according to the author, when Jesus proclaimed that all men are equal, during his studies among these Hindus, the wrath of his hosts was aroused. They planned to kill him, but he fled to safety. Jesus continued to study among other Asian peoples, this report claims, until he returned to his homeland at the age of twenty-nine.

Other sources have considered the striking similarity between Zoroastrianism and the Judeo-Christian tradition. The question has been raised as to whether Jesus might have journeyed to Persia, where the Jews had twice been exiled centuries before Jesus was born.

Zoroaster lived about 500 years before Jesus. The Zoroastrian conception of the deity is strongly related to that of Judaism in that both are monotheistic. Although the two religions developed independently, there was undoubtedly cross-fertilization between them. It is also possible that early Christian thinking was influenced by Zoroastrianism directly.

For Zoroastrianism is a dualistic religion in which the forces of good and evil are pitted against each other. These forces are personified—much as they were to be in Christianity—as angels and archangels versus demons and archfiends. Zoroastrianism also includes belief in a final judgment and even in the concept of resurrection.

It is possible that Jesus was exposed to Hinduism, Buddhism, and Zoroastrianism. The strong similarity between the latter and the Judeo-Christian tradition led anthropologists and scholars of ancient history to search for and eventually prove cross-fertilization. As far as the legends that Jesus studied Hinduism and Buddhism are concerned, these remain unproven.

Other apocryphal sources have suggested that Jesus traveled to Egypt, Greece, and even Britain. Again, if these stories had any basis in fact, Jesus undoubtedly would have been familiar with the religious beliefs of these places.

The Egyptian religion included the story of Osiris, the hero who was resurrected after his death. In Egyptian mythology, Osiris, who was judge of the dead, was opposed by Set who eventually caused Osiris' death. Some sources indicate that Osiris' body was dismembered.

Jesus would have been exposed to Greek and Roman mythology in his homeland, where the influence of both cultures had been strong for a long time before Jesus' birth. Greek and Roman mythology contained many different gods. Naturally, the concept of many gods, or polytheism, was totally contrary to what Jews had believed since Abraham's day.

Other legends assert that, as a boy, Jesus journeyed to Britain, to the ancient land of the Druids. There is even a letter, reputedly written from St. Augustine to Pope Gregory the Great but probably forged, which claims that Jesus built a church in England. It states: "God beforehand acquainting them, [they] found a church constructed by no human art, but by the hands of Christ himself in the salvation of his people."[1]

According to the legend, Jesus visited Britain with Joseph of Arimathea, who was said to be his uncle. Joseph of Arimathea was a tin merchant, the story alleges. Britain was then the world's leading producer of tin, as it had been since the days of Julius Caesar. The legend claims that Joseph of Arimathea first landed at Cornwall with the young Jesus. They then went on to Glastonbury, where Jesus supposedly built a church.

If Jesus did really build a church at Glastonbury, this was about two centuries before the first known churches. The term, "church," originally meant the body of assembled believers in Jesus who followed The Way before they were called Christians. They met in Jewish synagogues and other places after the new faith was started. When the break came with Judaism, and synagogues could no longer be used by those following Jesus, the followers of The Way met in homes. It was only around 200 AD that buildings began to be erected to house the faithful in worship, and that the term acquired the additional meaning of an actual building.

In another legend which ties in with Jesus' alleged visit to Britain, Joseph of Arimathea is said to have returned to Britain after Jesus' death with the cup which Jesus used at the Last Supper. This drinking goblet, called the Holy Grail, became the object of innumerable quests by knights of the Round Table who served under King Arthur.

There are claims that King Arthur was a direct descendant of Joseph of Arimathea. Indeed, a marker at the Glastonbury ruins would seem to indicate King Arthur's grave. But the famous king is, himself, a semi-legendary figure, though an actual King Arthur probably led the ancient Britons against the Anglo-Saxon invaders.

As we'll see later in this book, Joseph of Arimathea had prepared a tomb for himself at Jerusalem. He gave this unused sepulcher or burial vault for Jesus' interment. According to the Glastonbury legends, Joseph of Arimathea returned to Britain and was buried there.

This legend can be found as early as the fifth century. Maelgwyn of Avalon wrote, around 540 AD, that the body of "St. Joseph" was buried at what had been the wattle church that the boy Jesus had started. In 1367, a monk named R. de Boston was quoted as saying, "The bodies of Joseph of Arimathea and his companions were found at Glastonbury."[2] In 1345, Edward III is said to have permitted a search for Joseph of Arimathea's body at Glastonbury. In 1577, Holinshed's *Chronicles* indicated that Joseph's tomb was at Glastonbury.[3] In 1662, John Ray noted in his *Itinerary*, "We saw Joseph of Arimathea's tomb and chapel at the end of the church."

And finally, in 1928, what were said to be the remains of Joseph of Arimathea were transferred to nearby St. Catherine's Chapel at Glastonbury.[4]

Obviously, this doesn't prove that Joseph of Arimathea was really buried in Britain, or that he was a tin merchant, or even that he brought Jesus as a boy to this island. But if Jesus did visit Britain before he began his public ministry, he would almost surely have encountered another religious group called the Druids.

This was an order of priests in very ancient times who were active in Gaul (ancient France) and Britain. The Druids existed at least two centuries before Jesus' time. Julius Caesar claims they originated in Britain. Three other writers (Diodorus Siculus, Athenaeus, and Strabo) wrote about the religious order called Druids. These prophets, sorcerers, and priests, popular in Welsh and Irish legends, later disappeared with the onset of Christianity.

All of Jesus' supposed travels would have brought him into contact with the major religious beliefs of his day. The apocryphal stories about the wanderings of Jesus seem to be attempting to find a way in which he could have been exposed to the religious beliefs of other peoples.

But, as we shall see, nothing in the Gospels gives any hint that Jesus ever traveled anywhere outside of his own small country. He never said anything which could be directly associated with the teachings of any

of these religious groups, with the possible exception of
Zoroastrianism. The similarities between Christianity
and Zoroastrianism have already been mentioned, with
one exception: Zoroaster was crucified.

The many stories about Jesus found outside the
Gospels include a number of so-called gnostic texts.
Several of these, *The Gospel of Truth* and *The Gospel
of Thomas,* were discovered in a gnostic library in Egypt
and are known as the Nag Hammadi Manuscripts.
Gnosticism had been known principally through the
writings of Christian critics of the gnostic religious convictions. Gnosticism, a form of mysticism which emphasized magic, collided with orthodox Christianity
during the Middle Ages and was considered a heresy.
However, although gnosticism entered Christianity at a
certain stage, it actually originated in ancient Egypt.

The *Gospel of Thomas* has some sayings reputedly
by Jesus, but since it is undoubtedly a forgery which was
written long after the death of the apostles, we will not
discuss it here.

In conclusion, then, there is no proof that Jesus was
ever out of Galilee between the ages of twelve and
thirty. However, since some of these stories have not
been proven false, they should be considered in our
search for the historical Jesus.

While most of these stories attempt to explain how
Jesus developed his later powers, they deal largely with
possible contacts he had with other religious groups.
But one source which claims to have knowledge about
Jesus' life that is not covered in the New Testament
touches on a question that intrigues some people: Was
there ever any romance in Jesus' life?

Yes, according to a volume called *Urantia.* According to this source, when Jesus was living in Nazareth a young woman fell in love with him. She is identified as Rebecca, the "eldest daughter of Ezra, a wealthy
merchant and trader of Nazareth."[5] However, Jesus
chose not to marry, the story says.

There are many other unsubstantiated legends
about Jesus which have no basis in the Gospels. These
include a childhood birthday party and a fanciful ac-

count of the boy Jesus riding a moonbeam. But many of these apocryphal accounts are not well known. They prove nothing; neither do they disprove anything. They just exist, and many have been kept alive for centuries by people who see something in them worth keeping.

To those who scoff at such possibilities, it is well to remember that about eighteen years of Jesus' life are not accounted for in the New Testament, and yet obviously Jesus did *something* in those years; he was *somewhere*. The Gospel of Saint John concludes with an intriguing suggestion:

> And there are also many other things which Jesus did, which if they were written in detail, I suppose that even the world itself would not contain the books which were written. (John 21:24)

We leave the mysterious silence of the missing years and turn to the record of Matthew, Mark, Luke, and John, who tell how Jesus began his ministry after the prophet John the Baptist prepared the way.

6

HISTORICAL
BACKGROUND
OF THE GOSPELS

Let us return to the time of Jesus so that we can
see it as it was then. It's a picture rarely presented to
modern readers.

It was a world in which both Greek and Roman
influence was tremendous. There were magnificent
Greek structures towering over the simple mud-brick
homes of the Jews. The very temple in which the Jews
worshipped God was Grecian in style. It had been
started about fifty years before the birth of Jesus by
King Herod who had a passion for Hellenistic culture.
The thirty-five-acre temple and grounds would not be
finished for another forty years.

King Herod was long dead by the time Jesus began
his ministry. He had died horribly of an extremely painful stomach ailment a few days after killing his third
son who had aspired to the throne. That had been
about thirty years before. But Herod's monuments to
his love of Greek culture still stood in rigid splendor all
over Jerusalem and throughout Palestine. It had been
the king's desire to endow this province of Rome with
a splendor which would stir the admiration of everyone.
So the man who loved the beauty of Greece and the

power of Rome had stamped the culture of the Jews with his own individual brand of Hellenism.

In this, he always took care to honor the emperor by whose authority he had almost total control over his province. And though Herod had been careful to offend neither the sense of modesty nor the religious convictions of the Jews, he did many things the Jews didn't like.

He had, for example, erected a huge sports hippodrome southeast of the temple. The Jews were naturally offended because wrestling there was performed nude in the Greek style. Near the hippodrome, but slightly to its west, there was a theater which also featured displays offensive to the Jews. But there were also several synagogues in addition to the temple.

There were synagogues all over Palestine, which was divided into tetrarchies as part of a province under the control of Syria. A tetrarch ruled the Roman political division called a tetrarchy. However, Judea, in which Jerusalem was located, didn't have a tetrarch. A stronger man was needed there, so a procurator or governor had charge although he didn't live in Jerusalem.

The Romans had built a viaduct across the Kidron Valley. The viaduct extended beyond the temple, which used lots of water in connection with the continual animal sacrifices, to Herod's fortified palace. It stood on the extreme western edge of the city. After Jerusalem was destroyed in 70 AD, nothing remained of the temple and the surrounding walls of the city except the western wall, since called the Wailing Wall, which was part of Herod's palace.

To the north of the temple, with its handsome columns and Hellenistic portico, or covered porch, the Roman procurator's combined palace and fortress stood against the Jerusalem wall. The imposing Tower of Antonia was here, along with a wide stone pavement on which the Roman cohorts could assemble and the cavalry parade could pass in review.

The Roman procurator could also have his great chair brought there to sit in judgment of those brought before him. He was the Roman official in charge of administering a minor province. Sometimes he was called governor. He was certain to be a Roman as a result of the emperor's unpleasant experience with the ethnarch, Archelaus. Although Palestine was under the province of Syria, it was still best to have a strong procurator in the principal Jewish city. The governor didn't have to live there, but on special occasions, when the Jews were most likely to cause trouble, the procurator led his armed troops into Jerusalem to prevent or put down civil disturbances.

That sometimes meant thousands of crosses around the city, outside the walls, where the corpses were left unless ransomed.

The best way to see Jerusalem was from the Mount of Olives, across the Kidron Valley to the east of the temple. In fact, the Eastern Gate led directly to the mountain on which centuries of Jews had lit signal fires to announce that the official sighting of the new or full moon had been made.

From this mountain, with the trees which gave it its name, and the little villages of Bethany and Bethphage, it was possible to look down onto the splendid majesty of the temple, the solemn Tower of Antonia, and the Grecian beauty of Herod's palace.

Not far from the procurator's palace-fortress, but across a moat to protect the city from attack on that side, the legionnaires had their camp. As a rule, they stayed pretty much out of sight, for the Jews had never ceased to resist the occupation forces. There was a movement developing which featured Jewish fanatics with daggers. They struck in crowds, often killing a Roman or another person considered offensive to their nation. The assassins, as the Romans called these zealously patriotic Jews, then disappeared in the crowd.

In the midst of this tension-filled world, in which Roman public baths in richly-decorated buildings stood next to synagogues, and in which Greek could be heard almost as often as the Aramaic spoken by the Jews, there was sickness, disease, and poverty.

A rich Jew might have a mosaic tile floor, but almost everyone else had dirt floors. The houses were simple, square, functional, with few, if any, windows. The flat roof had a parapet so people wouldn't fall off when they walked there in the cool of the evening. The streets of Jerusalem were narrow, crooked, and filled with the wastes which naturally accumulated from animals and human beings. The city walls and man-made moat which surrounded Jerusalem prevented easy approach or attack. And the city was filled with cisterns where precious water brought in by viaducts might be stored against siege. For the city had often been the target of aggressors.

The great King David himself had taken the city from the Jebusites about ten centuries before, entering through an underground waterway instead of fruitlessly assaulting the great stone walls. David had made Jerusalem his capital and expanded the empire all through the land God had promised Abraham long before David's time.

But outside the city walls, across the valleys, the Judean hills were full of bandits. The poor of the land, of various nationalities and tribes, had taken to a life of crime as a last resort against extreme poverty. Even King Herod had not been able to entirely subdue the outlaws who preyed on Jew and Gentile alike.

In those hills, too, were dogs and vultures. The dogs were wild, vicious beasts that joined the carrion birds in stripping clean the bones of the many crucified men that the Romans executed singly or by the thousands and left to rot on the crosses.

Beyond the hills, tucked into various places where there was water, Jewish villages clung to life. Sometimes a Roman general would enter with his troops and take everyone prisoner. The slave traders did a brisk business when the Romans sold off a whole village at once for some real or imagined wrong.

This, then, was the real world in which a Jew of Jesus' time was born. It wasn't a pretty world, for the beggars with their hideous sores lined the streets and the wailing of women bemoaning their dead punctuated the night's silence. But all of this suffering of a captive people lay beyond the ornateness of the temple, the

two palaces, and the other beautiful or impressive structures which marked the Graeco-Roman influence on a
distinctive culture the Jews were proud to call their
own. After all, they believed that God himself had
chosen them as a special people for a special work;
through them, all the nations of the world were to be
blessed.

There were some Jews who had accepted the forms
of Hellenism, such as shaving their beards or cutting
their hair short. Still, the majority of the Jews clung to
their own culture and religious faith.

And that faith included a belief in the coming of
the Messiah. Before he came, it was believed that someone else would prepare the way. Nobody knew who
would prepare the way, or who the Messiah was, or
when he would come; it was enough that he was coming
and that someone was coming before him to make
ready.

While they diverge in many other respects, all four
Gospel writers felt that it was important to set down
facts about John the Baptist, since it was he who prepared the way for Jesus. Only when John the Baptist's
work is explained can the four Gospel writers bring
Jesus the adult into the scene.

Luke also felt it was important to record historical
facts as a background to introducing John the Baptist.
As always, Luke had a purpose. He was a Gentile
writing to another non-Jew. The recipient of Luke's
letter was an intelligent person. The Greek physician
knew that his story of Jesus would have more credibility
if he could pinpoint the year when it began.

It was a risk, for if Luke was proven wrong about
his historical data, he could be criticized for the rest of
his reporting. In fact, Luke's whole story would be suspect. But on the other hand, if Luke could establish his
authority from the outset, what he had to say about
John the Baptist and Jesus would be acceptable to someone who lived far away but had heard about the strange
events in Palestine.

Luke has already said he has investigated everything and is going to report it in the order in which it happened. So the physician prefaces his introduction of Jesus the adult by touching on those facts which his reader already knows. His strategy is to establish a common ground between himself and his reader.

First, Luke declares that the events he will recount began in the fifteenth year of Tiberius Caesar's reign. This was when Pontius Pilate was governor of Judea and Herod Antipas was tetrarch of Galilee. Luke also mentions that at the time Philip, the brother of Herod Antipas, was tetrarch in the northern areas of Ituraea and Trachonitis. The third tetrarch was Lysanias, whose headquarters were in Abilene. This town was about twenty miles northwest of Damascus and attached to the city of Abila.

It was at this period of time, Luke declares,

> that the word of God come to John, son of Zacharias, in the wilderness. And he came into all the district around the Jordan, preaching a baptism of repentance for forgiveness of sins. (Luke 3:1–3)

How has Luke fared as a historian after nearly two thousand years?

Tiberius Caesar succeeded Caesar Augustus, the first Roman emperor, who died in 14 AD. Tiberius, Augustus' adopted son, had been co-regent the last ten years of the emperor's life. But if Luke was calculating on the basis of Tiberius' reign as emperor—not as co-regent—and his words would indicate that he was, then the fifteenth year of Tiberius' reign would have been in 29 AD.

This concurs with other historical data given by Luke. Pontius Pilate was the fifth Roman procurator, or governor—procurators having been established in Judea after Archelaus was deposed. Pilate's governorship of Judea, Samaria, and Idumea began in 26 AD. He would have been there three years when Luke's account of Jesus' emergence from the eighteen missing years begins.

The Herod whom Luke refers to as the tetrarch of Galilee was not King Herod, who was now dead, but Herod Antipas. He was brother of Archelaus, who had succeeded their infamous father, King Herod. Archelaus had been exiled by the emperor in 6 AD. Herod Antipas was not as bloodthirsty as his father or brother had been.

Philip, whom Luke mentions next, was the half-brother of Herod Antipas. They had the same father but different mothers. The Philip of Luke's account was tetrarch from 4 BC, when his father died, until 34 AD, when he himself died. His was a quiet, uneventful life.

Little is known of Lysanias. Josephus makes mention of an "Abila, which had been the tetrarchy of Lysanias."[1] A temple inscription at Abila, which has been dated as between 14 and 29 AD,[2] mentions "Lysanias the tetrarch." There are also some coins known to honor "Lysanias tetrarch and high priest." But there are other known historical men by the name of Lysanias, so the one Luke meant is in doubt. However, there is no question that a man by that name existed, and there was a tetrarchy at the same time. Luke should be given the benefit of the doubt as to the accuracy of the other names he mentions.

The last two persons Luke includes in his introduction to the story he is about to recount are the high priests, Annas and Caiaphas.

There could only be one high priest at a time. Josephus tells us that Annas had been high priest. He was such a powerful man that five of his sons, as well as his son-in-law, became high priest. It would appear that Annas was the honorary or titular high priest at the time Luke mentions and that Caiaphas was the actual high priest. In fact, it is known that Joseph Caiaphas, Annas' son-in-law, was high priest from about 18 to 36 AD.

Although the high priest technically held office for life, the Romans set up and deposed the high priest at will.

We will meet Pilate, Herod Antipas, and the two priests later in the story about Jesus. But for now, let us see why Luke was taking such elaborate precautions in introducing John the Baptist.

As Luke explains at the beginning of his Gospel, John was the son of Zacharias, an elderly priest, and his equally aged wife. Luke says that this birth was the result of an angel's promise. The child's name was to be John, and he was chosen of God for a special mission:

> He will go as a forerunner before Him in the spirit and power of Elijah, to turn the hearts of the fathers back to the children, and the disobedient to the attitude of the righteous; so as to make ready a people prepared for the Lord. (Luke 1:17)

The "word of the Lord" came to John in the "wilderness," where he had lived the life of a recluse. But even from his mother's womb, John had been "filled with the Holy Spirit." (Luke 3:2; 1:15)

John was an ascetic, one who renounces the comforts of life and practices strict self-discipline and self-denial. He had lived on locusts and wild honey, Matthew explains. John wore a simple garment of camel's hair with a leather belt. He might have looked a bit like a wild man with long hair and beard.

But what John said and did was enough to bring people from Jerusalem, down the steep, winding road to the Jordan River, braving heat and other inconveniences all the way. The following scene is a recreation of John the Baptist preaching and baptizing at the Jordan River.

John had stripped off his outer garment and had waded waist-deep into the water. His white undergarment thoroughly covered his chest so as not to offend the Jewish sense of modesty.

As he had for days, John the Baptist raised his voice and called to the crowds on shore. "Repent, for the kingdom of heaven is at hand!"

The crowd stood motionless, listening to the message of the speaker.

"Repent! One is coming after me who is greater than I. I am not even fit to untie his sandals. I baptize you with water, but he will baptize you with the Holy Spirit."

The crowd stirred uneasily. As John built up to his invitation, there were many who looked anxiously at their friends and then decided. They would wade into the waters that flowed down from snowy Mount Hermon, and they would be baptized as a sign they had repented of their sins and would turn from them.

But not all those who came were so willing to wade out to the man who was baptizing with water. Some of the priests came the long, hard, winding way from Jerusalem to the hot Jordan plains area to ask questions of John.

"Who are you?"

It was one of the questions that the Pharisees would have asked. The Pharisees were a sect who considered themselves the elect. They were purists who, in their day, were somewhat like the Puritans of England and early America. The Pharisees believed in keeping to the letter of the Law as a way of getting closer to God.

The Sadducees, the second of the three principal Jewish sects, would also have wanted to know about who John really was. The Sadducees disagreed with the Pharisees on such issues as whether there was an afterlife and whether there were angels. But both groups believed in the Messiah.

Some people said John the Baptist acted like an Essene, the third major Jewish religious sect. The Essenes had withdrawn from the mainstream of life to form their own community near the Qumran caves near the Dead Sea. They weren't even mentioned in the New Testament, but their writings came to light nearly 2000 years later. These writings, known as the Dead Sea

Scrolls, shed a whole new light on the final years before Jerusalem was destroyed.

The priests from Jerusalem cupped their hands and called from the bank to John the Baptist. "Are you the Messiah?"

Everyone strained to hear the answer. "I am not the Christ."

The murmurs indicated that the reaction to John's answer was mixed. But the priests were continuing their interrogation. "Who are you then? Elijah?"

"I am not."

Elijah was one of two men in the Jewish Scriptures who had never died. Enoch had been "translated" so that he didn't experience death. Elijah, on the other hand, had been taken to heaven in a fiery chariot. In the ninth century BC, Elijah, the prophet of the Northern Kingdom, had lived as a hermit. He had challenged the wicked Queen Jezebel, and had heard the "still, small voice of God." Elijah the Tishbite had left the earth in a unique way, and was expected to return before the Messiah came.

There was scriptural authority for this belief:

> Behold, I am going to send you Elijah
> the prophet before the coming of the great
> and terrible day of the Lord. (Mal. 4:5)

The crowds on the shores of the Jordan waited for the priests' next question to John the Baptist. "Are you the Prophet?"

This question recalled an ancient promise of the coming of the Messiah. Moses had assured the Israelites after coming down from Mount Sinai:

> The Lord your God will raise up for
> you a prophet like me from among you, from
> your countrymen. You shall listen to him.
> (Deut. 18:15)

To the people on Jordan's shore, John's answer resounded clear and simple. "No."

The priests were getting a little annoyed. If the wild-looking man in the river didn't claim to be either Elijah or the Messiah, then who was he?

They called again.

> Who are you, so that we may give an
> answer to those who sent us? What do you
> say about yourself? (John 1:22)

This was the question that everyone had been waiting to hear answered. They strained to hear the words from the holy man who stood in the center of the river. "I am 'the voice of one crying in the wilderness: Make straight the way of the Lord.' " (Isaiah 40: 3)

There it was! John the Baptist considered himself the forerunner of the Messiah! And if the forerunner was here, could the Christ be far behind?

The next day, after the priests had returned to Jerusalem with their answer, John was baptizing as usual when a most unusual thing happened. The long line of baptismal candidates had been coming to John, confessing their sins, being immersed and then leaving for the shore while others moved up. One of those who presented himself for baptism caused John to stop in surprise.

Jesus stood before John.

The baptizer shook his head at Jesus. "I have need to be baptized by you, and do you come to me?" (Matt. 3:14)

Jesus nodded. He spoke so softly that only those standing nearby could hear. *"Permit it at this time."* (Matt. 3:15)

John the Baptist hesitated a moment longer. Then, gazing deep into Jesus' eyes and seeing the conviction there, John bowed his head. Then John baptized Jesus.

As Jesus' head reappeared from the Jordan and water poured from his long dark hair and beard, a dove suddenly fluttered down from the sky. John recognized the Spirit of God as a dove descending to Jesus' shoulder. A voice from the opened heavens proclaimed:

"This is My beloved Son in whom I am well pleased."
(Matt. 3:17)

And so it was, as presented in the Gospels, that
Jesus of Nazareth reemerged. He was now about thirty
years old. He was ready to begin the work which was
to shape western civilization for 2,000 years.

But before he could reemerge, his way had to be
prepared by John the Baptist whose existence in the
Gospels is confirmed by historical records.

Let us look first at how John is presented in the
Gospels.

Matthew declares that shortly after John baptized
Jesus, John was thrown into prison. With the same
directness with which he had called some religious
leaders "serpents" while he preached in the Jordan,
John had condemned the marriage of Herod Antipas to
Herodias: "It is not lawful for you to have her." (Matt.
14:4)

He was right, according to Jewish law. Herodias,
King Herod's granddaughter, was the daughter of a
son whom Herod had executed. Herodias had divorced
Herod Philip and married his half-brother, Antipas.
Since Herodias was Antipas' niece, the marriage was
incestuous. Besides, Herodias had borne a child to
Philip. By Jewish law, a man could not marry his
brother's widow if the first union had resulted in a
child.

Herod Antipas was not as angry as Herodias about
John the Baptist's charges. She wasn't satisfied that
John was in prison, but plotted to have her husband
execute him.

The Gospels do not go into detail about why John
the Baptist was imprisoned. They simply mention the
incident relating to Herodias, and speak generally of
what Luke calls "the wicked things which Herod
[Antipas] had done." But Josephus confirms the New
Testament story, providing new details and a different
motive for the whole situation. The Jewish historian and
the Gospel writers concur in saying that John the

Baptist was executed as a result of Herodias' evil machinations.

The New Testament writers explain that Herodias planned a way to get John the Baptist killed. On her husband's birthday, she had her daughter dance before him and his guests. In a moment of male weakness, the pleased leader cried out to this stepdaughter that he would give her whatever she wanted as a reward for such dancing.

The girl sought her mother's counsel. Herodias told her daughter to return to Antipas and say, "Give me here on a platter the head of John the Baptist." (Matt. 14:8)

Matthew incorrectly refers to the tetrarch as king in writing that although Antipas "was grieved, the king commanded it to be given because of his oaths, and because of his dinner guests. And he sent and had John beheaded in the prison." (Matt. 14:9–10)

Josephus' account varies slightly. His history records that Herod slew him, who was a good man, and commanded the Jews to exercise virtue, both as to righteousness towards one another, and piety toward God, and so to come to baptism; for that the washing would be acceptable to him, if they made use of it, not in order to the putting away of some sins, but for the purification of the body; supposing still that the soul was thoroughly purified beforehand by righteousness. . . . When others came to crowd about him, for they were greatly moved by hearing his words, Herod, who feared lest the great influence John had over the people might put it into his power and inclination to raise a rebellion (for they seemed ready to do anything he should advise), thought it best, by putting him to death, to prevent any mischief he might cause, and not bring himself into difficulties, by sparing a man who might make him repent of it when it should be too late.[3]

Josephus adds that Herod Antipas had John the Baptist made a prisoner because of his suspicious temperament. John was sent to Macherus, a castle near the Arabian border, and there put to death.

The Jewish chronicler indicates that the reason he

included John the Baptist in his history is that Herod Antipas' army was later destroyed when his former father-in-law, Aretas, king of Arabia, attacked the tetrarch because it was his daughter whom Antipas had divorced in order to marry Herodias. Josephus adds that some of the Jews attributed the destruction of Herod's army to the wrath of God over what he had done to John.[4]

In addition to confirming the existence of John the Baptist, Josephus gives us the name of the famous dancer who cost John the Baptist his head. She was Salome, who later married her uncle Philip II—her father having been Philip I or Herod Philip—the tetrarch of Gaulanitis, Trachonitis, Batanaea, and Panias.

For Matthew, the beginning of Jesus' ministry coincides wth the imprisonment of John the Baptist. "Now when he [Jesus] heard that John had been taken into custody, he withdrew into Galilee; and leaving Nazareth, he came and settled in Capernaum, which is by the sea, in the region of Zebulun and Naphtali." (Matt. 4:12–13) This was to fulfill the ancient prophecy of Isaiah that the Christ would come from "beyond the Jordan, Galilee of the Gentiles." (Matt. 4:15)

Jesus began where John had left off, preaching: "Repent, for the kingdom of heaven is at hand." But Jesus soon went far beyond this, and entered upon a public ministry of healing, teaching, preaching, and performing miracles which led him into a direct confrontation with the most powerful political forces in the land.

7

CONFLICTS OVER
JESUS' MINISTRY

Everything Jesus did seemed to lead to conflict.
That was even true of his teaching.

He almost lost his life the first time he spoke in the
town of Nazareth. There, instead of sticking to the
message he had picked up from John the Baptist, Jesus
made a startling statement which resulted in a mob
reaction.

Luke, the Greek Gospel writer, sets the stage for
this violent encounter by declaring that Jesus "returned
to Galilee in the power of the Spirit; and news about
him spread through all the surrounding district." (Luke
4:14–15)

It was Jesus' custom to attend the synagogue on the
Sabbath. In the following scene, we will dramatize what
happened when Jesus entered the Nazareth synagogue.

Jesus stood up to read. The scroll of Isaiah was
handed to him. He opened the scroll, found the place
where the prophet had spoken about the coming of the
Messiah, and began to read aloud the ancient words:
*"The Spirit of the Lord is upon me, because he sent
me to proclaim release to the captives, and recovery of
sight to the blind, to set free those who are down-*

trodden, to proclaim the favorable year of the Lord."
(Luke 4:18–19)

Jesus returned the scroll to the attendant and sat
down, as was customary when commenting on the
Scriptures. All eyes in the synagogue focused on him as
he prepared to comment on the passage he had read.
To comment on the Scriptures was the prerogative of
any adult member of the synagogue. *"Today this Scripture has been fulfilled in your hearing."* (Luke 4:21)

The crowd responded: "Fulfilled? How can this
Scripture be fulfilled today? What's he saying?" The
reaction to such a declaration swelled to an audible
murmur: "That's blasphemy!" (Luke 4:28–29)

The Jews were an explosive people when it came
to their religion. They didn't want to hear anything
which was blasphemous or irreverent to their God. As
the Romans had discovered over and over, the Jews
could move quickly and in unison where their religious
beliefs were involved.

Jesus' listeners promptly reached the point of action. "Only the Messiah could make such a claim!"
(Luke 4:28)

The Gospels tell us that the protesting congregation
rose as one and advanced on Jesus. He was ejected
from the synagogue and hustled toward a cliff outside
of Nazareth. Jesus was about to face death by stoning,
the punishment for blasphemy.

But, in some way the Gospels treat as an unexplained mystery, Jesus escaped the mob. He passed
"through their midst," Luke explains, and "went his
way." (Luke 4:30)

Jesus left his home town of Nazareth. He went to
live at Capernaum by the Sea of Galilee. He gathered
twelve disciples and began training them to carry on
the work he had started.

Only four of these disciples are important to our
story: James and John (the sons of Zebedee), Simon
Peter, and Judas Iscariot. The first three were Galilean
fishermen. Judas was probably the only Judean among
the twelve. Nothing is told of his background, except

that he was from Kerioth, a town not now clearly identified, and that he was the son of Simon Iscariot.

Peter was known for his blunt, outspoken manner. Peter, James, and John became the three closest to Jesus. Judas eventually betrayed his leader.

Jesus' teachings were sometimes to the multitudes and sometimes to a single individual. To the groups who came to hear him, Jesus offered hope in what are called the Beatitudes:

Blessed are the poor in spirit, for theirs is the kingdom of heaven. Blessed are those who mourn, for they shall be comforted. (Matt. 5:3–4)

Jesus assured the people they were of great value to God and man. *"You are the salt of the earth . . ."* and *"You are the light of the world . . ."* Jesus added, *"Do not be afraid, little flock, for your Father has chosen to give you the kingdom."* (Luke 12:32)

Jesus had begun by declaring: *"The kingdom of heaven is at hand."* (Matt. 4:17) He clarified that to mean: *"The kingdom of heaven is within you."* (Luke 17:21)

Often Jesus preached to a single individual, as was the case with Nicodemus. He was not a likely candidate for conversion, for Nicodemus was a Pharisee, a member of the ruling Sanhedrin, and probably rich. The Sanhedrin was a body of about 70 Jews who had authority over religious matters, and who could decide whether a person should be put to death. The Romans, however, reserved the right to conduct executions.

Nicodemus was afraid to be seen talking to Jesus, so he came by night. The visitor began the conversation by admitting he was convinced Jesus was no ordinary person.

Nicodemus said, "Rabbi, we know that you have come from God as a teacher; for no one can do these things that you do unless God is with him." (John 3:1–2)

Jesus replied, *"I say to you, unless one is born again, he cannot see the kingdom of God."* (John 3:3)

Nicodemus, a practical man, asked how a man who is old could be born again. Jesus explained that he meant one must be *"born of water and the spirit"* if he wanted to enter the kingdom of God. (John 3:5)

The discussion continued for some time with Jesus marveling that Nicodemus could be *"a teacher of Israel, and yet not understand these things."* (John 3:10) Jesus added, *"If I told you earthly things and you do not believe, how shall you believe if I tell you heavenly things?"* (John 3:12)

The Gospels include only one more incident about Nicodemus until the final confrontation between Jesus and his opponents. But the words of Jesus to the Pharisee who came to him by night remain proverbial today. In a Gallup Poll, something like half of those who were interviewed claimed they had been "born again." Jimmy Carter, President of the United States, used that term while running as a candidate for the nation's highest office.

But Jesus' teachings were not always so uncontroversial. As his reputation grew, so did his opposition. It was natural that those who challenged his teachings would be those who considered themselves knowledgeable in the Jewish laws and traditions.

The Pharisees were strict legalists. So when Jesus' disciples walked through a grainfield on the Sabbath and picked some heads of grain, the Pharisees asked Jesus: "Why are they doing what is not lawful on the Sabbath?" (Mark 2:23) Jesus replied that King David had once eaten the sacred or consecrated bread although it was lawful only for the priests. Jesus summed up his viewpoint by declaring: *"The Sabbath was made for man, and not man for the Sabbath. Consequently, the Son of Man is Lord even of the Sabbath."* (Mark 2:27–28) The Gospel of Saint Mark doesn't say how the Pharisees responded to Jesus' answer. Although he often openly challenged their authority, his mastery over scriptural tradition made it difficult for them to accuse him of any outright crime. Jesus often refers to himself as the "Son of Man."

But as more and more people followed Jesus, more and more religious leaders began to oppose him. It may be that some genuinely believed that he was violating the Mosaic laws which they had been entrusted with keeping. But many were frightened that, as a result of his power as a popular leader, their own authority would be challenged by the people.

Soon his detractors were trying to find ways to trap Jesus. An opportunity seemed to have been found when the religious leaders caught a woman in the act of adultery. Nothing is said about the man involved. The woman was brought to Jesus.

The accusers were attempting to entangle Jesus in an unresolvable dilemma in which he would have to choose between being merciful and following the dictates of the Mosaic Law. The scribes and Pharisees set the woman before Jesus and framed their question.

"Teacher, in the Law, Moses commanded us to stone such women; what do you say?"

Jesus answered, *"He who is without sin among you, let him be the first to throw a stone at her."*

It was such a profound reply that gradually all the woman's accusers drifted away. Only Jesus and the woman remained. Jesus asked, *"Did no one condemn you?"*

"No one, Lord," the woman answered.

Jesus assured her, *"Neither do I condemn you; go your way; from now on sin no more."* (John 8:5–11)

Jesus taught compassion in moral as well as religious matters. After all, who was without sin?

Jesus' teachings brought him into conflict with the small, powerful group called the Sadducees.

The Sadducees believed that there was no resurrection of the body after death, while the Pharisees did believe in resurrection. The Scriptures were unclear on that point. There had been suggestions of a life after death in the Old Testament writings, but it wasn't until after the Babylonian exile that resurrection of the dead became acceptable to some Jews, such as the Pharisees, while others, such as the Sadducees, continued to deny it.

The Sadducees confronted Jesus with the hypothetical situation of seven brothers who married the same woman in succession. Each of the brothers had died childless. Under Mosaic law, the surviving brother or a close male kinsman was obliged to marry the woman and rear children as the deceased brother's own.

But, the Sadducees concluded their made-up story, "all seven left no offspring. Last of all the woman died, too. In the resurrection, when they will rise again, which one's wife will she be?" (Mark 12:22–23)

Jesus replied that the Sadducees didn't understand the Scriptures, or the power of God. When they rise from the dead, *"they neither marry, nor are given in marriage, but are like angels in heaven."* (Mark 12:25)

However, Jesus added, citing one of Moses' conversations with God, *"He is not the God of the dead, but of the living."* (Mark 12:27)

Jesus had several discussions about the resurrection of the dead. This was not the same as raising someone from the dead and returning them to life on this earth. That had happened a couple of times in the Old Testament. Jesus had also restored a couple of people to life by this time. He meant there was a life beyond this one, plus a judgment which would find the just rewarded and the others punished. It wasn't just "bad" people like murderers who failed to make heaven. Jesus explained: *"Not everyone who says to me, 'Lord, Lord,' will enter the kingdom of heaven; but he who does the will of my Father who is in heaven."* (Matt. 7:21)

Not only acts of commission but acts of omission as well might send a person to hell. And, Jesus made it clear, some of the people were going to be surprised at being denied entrance to heaven.

Jesus was forthright in dealing with the reality of hell. He warned that anyone who was angry with his brother, but not reconciled, or said, "You fool!" was guilty enough to go into the fires of hell.

Jesus' bluntness in speech about the judgment extended to the scribes and Pharisees. Jesus pronounced woes on them and then added, *"You serpents! You brood of vipers! How shall you escape the sentence of hell?"* (Matt. 23:33)

But, Jesus had explained to Nicodemus, *"God so loved the world that He gave His only begotten son, that whoever believes in him should not perish, but have eternal life."* (John 3:16)

Heaven and hell were real, but it was not God's choice that anyone should suffer in the afterlife. It was each individual's free choice: each could make his or her own decision about the two alternatives open in eternity.

While the question of life after death was treated ambiguously in the Old Testament, Jesus' teachings on this subject were designed to make it clear that those who believe in him should also have everlasting life. The conviction that death was not absolute became a pivotal point in Jesus' teachings that continues to this day.

But there was one more important aspect to Jesus' teachings about what would happen after he died. He would come again. He declared:

"In my Father's house are many dwelling places; if it were not so, I would have told you; for I go to prepare a place for you. And if I go and prepare a place for you, I will come again, and receive you to myself, that where I am, there you may be also." (John 14:2–3)

Naturally, at that time, the disciples did not understand what Jesus meant. Nor did they understand when he told them the time was coming when not one stone of the temple would be left standing. (Matt. 24:2) However, when they had left the city and were sitting on the Mount of Olives, the disciples privately asked him a question. "Tell us, when will these things be, and what will be the sign of your coming, and of the end of the age?" (Matt. 24:3)

Jesus gave a long answer concerning the Last Judgment and heralding his Second Coming. Jesus concluded his narrative of the events which would be signs of his Second Coming by declaring: *They will see the Son of Man coming on the clouds of the sky with power and great glory. And he will send forth his angels with a great trumpet and they will gather together his elect from the four winds, from one end of the sky to the other.* (Matt. 24:5–31)

For about three and a half years, Jesus continued to teach and perform miracles. No matter what he did, he seemed to stir up opposition in all but a few cases, such as his healing of Mary Magdalene. She became a faithful follower of Jesus, and is one of the most fascinating women of the New Testament.

Among the Gospel writers, only Luke gives any hint of how Jesus met this remarkable woman. Luke only tells us that as Jesus went from one city to another, "proclaiming and preaching the kingdom of God," he healed Mary Magdalene. Luke writes: "And also some women who had been healed of evil spirits and sickness: Mary who was called Magdalene, from whom seven devils had gone out." (Luke 8:2)

Often, when Jesus came into conflict with the authorities, it seemed as though he would be finally put to death. But "his hour was not yet come," the Gospels repeatedly assure us. (John 7:30; 8:20) However, it came closer with each encounter between the worker of miracles and the religious leaders who felt that their laws and traditions were threatened by Jesus. For example, when Jesus healed a blind man, the religious leaders put the man out of the synagogue because of his belief that the miracle had been performed by a man sent by God.

There were episodes such as the day Jesus walked under Solomon's portico at the temple and angered the religious leaders. They had demanded, "How long will you keep us in suspense? If you are the Christ, tell us plainly!" (John 10:24)

Jesus answered, *"I told you, and you do not believe . . . I and the Father are one."* (John 10:25, 29)

The Jews had taken up stones to kill him for blasphemy: "Because you, being a man, make yourself out to be God." (John 10:33)

The accumulation of such episodes underlined the inevitability of what was to come. Luke declares, "And it came about, when the days were approaching for his ascension, that he resolutely set his face to go to Jerusalem." (Luke 9:51)

Only Jesus knew what was going to happen there. He made sure his identity as the Messiah was known to his inner circle of disciples, and then he predicted his death.

He began by asking, *"Who do people say that I am?"* They replied, "John the Baptist; and others say Elijah; but still others, one of the prophets."

Jesus then asked, *"But who do you say that I am?"* Peter answered, "You are the Christ." (Matt. 16:13–16)

Strangely, it seemed, Jesus warned them not to tell anyone. Matthew reports, "Then he warned the disciples that they should tell no one that he was the Christ." (Matt. 16:20)

Jesus next tried to prepare the disciples for what was to happen. Matthew declares that Jesus "began to show his disciples that he must go to Jerusalem, and suffer many things from the elders and chief priests and scribes, and be killed, and be raised up on the third day." (Matt. 16:21)

The disciples not only didn't understand, but Peter took it upon himself to rebuke Jesus. "God forbid it, Lord! This shall never happen to you." (Matt. 16:22)

The disciples, like many other people who had followed Jesus during the time of his ministry, were convinced not only that he was the Messiah but that he was going to set up a new kingdom in Jerusalem. To even his closest disciples, such as Peter, the idea that Jesus should go to Jerusalem to die was in contradiction with their concept of the Messiah.

Jesus tried to prepare the inner circle of disciples six days after Peter rebuked Jesus. He took Peter, James, and John to a mountain where they saw him transfigured before them. Matthew explains that Jesus' face shone like the sun and his clothes became as white as light.

The three startled apostles saw Jesus talking with

the two prophets, Moses and Elijah. The former, according to the Bible, had been buried by God before the Hebrews crossed the Jordan toward Jericho and the Promised Land. Elijah had gone to heaven in a whirlwind, and had never died.

When the scene faded, and Jesus was himself again, with only the three disciples, Peter opened his mouth and proposed building three tabernacles or memorials at the site: one for Jesus, the others for Elijah and Moses.

While Peter was still speaking, Matthew declares, "a bright cloud overshadowed them; and behold, a voice out of the cloud, saying, 'This is My beloved Son, with whom I am well pleased; hear him!' " (Matt. 17:5)

The disciples fell on their faces in fear. But Jesus reassured them and warned them, *"Tell the vision to no one until the Son of Man has risen from the dead."* (Matt. 17:9)

So Jesus continued his journey, leaving Galilee, passing Samaria, arriving at Jericho, and starting the long, hard climb to Jerusalem and death. For inside the city, a conspiracy to take Jesus' life had been going on since at least the previous October.

It would take just one event for the plotters to be successful in their attempt on Jesus' life.

It came about in a rather unexpected way.

The Gospel of Saint John introduces the situation: "Now a certain man was ill, Lazarus of Bethany, the village of Mary and her sister Martha." (John 11:1)

Although the Gospel of Saint John had not previously mentioned this family, Luke had introduced them earlier in his narrative. Jesus and his disciples had been invited by Martha to share her hospitality. The home was apparently hers. While Martha served, her sister Mary used to sit and listen to Jesus. Lazarus was their brother, John says, but Luke is silent on that point. However, in the course of his travels, Jesus had often been to their home.

Jesus loved Martha, Mary, and Lazarus, the

Scripture explains. So the sisters sent word to Jesus that "he whom you love is ill."

Yet Jesus delayed two days after receiving word of the illness. Then he told his disciples, *"Let us go into Judea again."* (John 11:7)

This frightened the apostles. "Rabbi, the Jews were but now seeking to stone you, and you are going there again?" (John 11:8)

Jesus explained that there were only twelve hours of light in a day, and that he must act while it was light. So Jesus assured the disciples, *"Our friend Lazarus has fallen asleep, but I go to awaken him."* (John 11:11)

The disciples didn't understand that Jesus meant Lazarus had died, so Jesus told them plainly: *"Lazarus is dead."* (John 11:14) So they set off for the village on the side of the Mount of Olives, about two miles outside of Jerusalem.

Someone ran ahead and told the sisters that Jesus was coming. Martha went to meet him, but Mary stayed in their home with grieving friends.

Martha gently reproved Jesus, "Lord, if you had been here, my brother would not have died." (John 11:21) She was thoughtful a moment and then added hopefully, "And even now I know that whatever you ask from God, God will give you."

Jesus replied, *"Your brother will rise again."* (John 11:23)

Martha said to Jesus: "I know that he will rise again in the resurrection at the last day." (John 11:24)

Jesus replied softly, *"I am the resurrection and the life. He who believes in me, though he die, yet shall he live, and whoever lives and believes in me shall never die. Do you believe this?"* (John 11:25)

Martha looked up through her tears and nodded. "Yes, Lord; I believe that you are the Christ, the Son of God, he who is coming into the world."

Mary joined Jesus and Martha. A tearful reunion was held before Jesus asked where Lazarus had been buried. They led him to a cave which had been sealed with a huge rolling stone.

Jesus commanded: *"Take away the stone."* (John 11:39)

Martha protested in a whisper. "He's been dead four days; there will be an odor!" (John 11:39)

"Didn't I tell you that if you would believe," Jesus reminded her, "you would see the glory of God?" (John 11:40)

So they took away the stone.

Then Jesus lifted up his eyes toward the heavens and said: *"Father, I thank You that You have heard me. I know that You always hear me, but I have said this because of the people standing by; that they may believe You did send me."* (John 11:41)

Then Jesus said in a loud voice: *"Lazarus! Come out!"* (John 11:43)

The sisters, their friends, and the disciples looked into the open blackness of the tomb. There was no sound, no movement as Jesus' words faded away into the Mount of Olives. And then, slowly, almost as though it were something imagined and not seen, there was a movement in the darkened tomb's interior.

In a moment, Lazarus shuffled slowly from the sepulcher's gloom into the full light of the day.

Lazarus was bound in the traditional burial clothes, which consisted of a simple white shroud plus a binding around hands and feet and a chinstrap which was used to keep the corpse's mouth shut.

Amid the gasps of the startled spectators, Jesus' quiet voice ordered, *"Unbind him and let him go."* (John 11:1–44)

Many of the watching Jews believed at that moment that Jesus was the Messiah. But other spectators hurried off to report to the Pharisees.

The raising of Lazarus prompted the religious leaders to gather in solemn assembly to discuss what action they could take. They met in the council-chamber of the Sanhedrin, in a large stone building with the seats arranged in a semi-circle facing the high priest who governed the highest tribunal of the Jews under the Romans.

Joseph Caiaphas presided but allowed the members to speak first. One cried, "What are we going to do? This man does many miracles!" (John 11:47)

Another spoke vehemently. "If we let him alone, all men will soon believe in him; and the Romans will come and take away both our place and our nation!" (John 11:48)

The high priest cleared his throat. "You don't know anything at all." (John 11:49)

The council members calmed down and turned expectantly to hear what the most powerful one among them was thinking.

"Consider this," Caiaphas suggested, then paused to thoughtfully stroke his gray beard. The council members leaned forward as the high priest swept them with his dark, thoughtful eyes. He was a shrewd man, they knew. He had a way of getting along with the Romans, by whose authority he held office.

"Consider what is expedient for us," Caiaphas resumed, "that one man should die for the people, so that the whole nation doesn't perish." (John 11:50)

The Jews did not lightly condemn a man to death. Even though the council had no authority to enact capital punishment, they rarely sought a judgment that a man was worthy of death, for life was a gift of God and only blasphemy and other high crimes were considered worthy of death.

There were some present who heard the high priest's suggestion with dismay. Perhaps Nicodemus was among those present, but the Gospels do not say. If Joseph of Arimathea was present, the Gospel writers do not indicate that he spoke.

But before anyone else could speak, a Sanhedrin member who had already mentally concurred with Caiaphas' views warned, "Not during the Passover feast! That might cause a riot! Some people consider Jesus a prophet!" (Matt. 26:5)

The council members nodded sagely. The city was filled with Jews who had come to the Passover. Pontius Pilate and his troops would be ready for trouble, for the Jews had repeatedly demonstrated during this event.

Many had died in past Passover riots. The religious leaders only wanted Jesus' life. That could be taken quietly, if handled correctly. They agreed among themselves to have Jesus arrested.

The council meeting broke up.

Now it was just a matter of time before they arrested Jesus. But how could that be done quietly? It could be done by bribing one of his disciples: Judas Iscariot.

8

THE FINAL DAYS
OF JESUS' LIFE

Only the Gospel of Saint John tells about the
dramatic moment when Judas Iscariot decided to betray
his leader. John explains:

> Jesus, therefore, six days before the Pass-
> over, came to Bethany where Lazarus was,
> whom Jesus had raised from the dead. So
> they made him a supper, and Martha was
> serving, but Lazarus was one of those reclin-
> ing at the table with him. (John 12:12)

This wasn't the first time the family had opened
their Bethany village home to Jesus. He and the
disciples had been their guests in previous visits to
Jerusalem, for their home was about two miles east of
the city, on the Mount of Olives. However, this was
certainly the most joyous occasion.

Mary of Bethany entered the room and approached
Jesus. She took a pound of very expensive spikenard
ointment and began anointing Jesus' bare feet. As the
rich perfume filled the simple room, Judas Iscariot
spoke up:

"Why was this ointment not sold for three hundred denarii, and given to poor people?" (John 12:5)

John explains that Judas, the only non-Galilean among the twelve disciples, acted as treasurer for the band. But he was stealing from the common purse.

Jesus looked up from where Mary of Bethany was anointing his feet with the costly ointment. Jesus' eyes fixed on Judas Iscariot's. *"Let her alone in order that she may keep it for the day of my burial. For the poor are always with you. But you do not always have me."* (John 12:7–8)

It is possible that it was this rebuke, delivered in front of the guests and other disciples, which stung Judas to action. John here suggests that Judas was already intending to betray his leader. But from this moment on, Judas was committed. The rebuke had brought him to a point where Judas' mind was made up. From now on, he'd wait and watch for an opportunity to turn Jesus over to the religious authorities. And if Judas was right in his expectations, he could get paid for the job.

Jesus began his last week of life with what has become known as the triumphal entry into Jerusalem. All four Gospels record that this dramatic incident took place on a Sunday morning, the first day of the Jewish week. Two disciples had gone, on Jesus' request, to bring back a donkey. The disciples threw their cloaks on the little animal and Jesus mounted. A multitude joyfully greeted the disciples and Jesus as they turned away from the Mount of Olives and headed for Jerusalem.

Matthew hails this event as another Old Testament prophecy fulfilled. He quotes the prophet Zechariah who lived in the first half of the sixth century BC: "Behold, your king is coming to you, gentle and mounted upon a donkey; even upon a colt, the foal of a beast of burden." (Matt. 21:5)

The procession became noisier as it wound down to the foot of the mountain and started across the Kidron Valley. Some excited spectators had obtained palm fronds to wave like banners before the man they expected to liberate them. Other people spread their cloaks in the path so that the donkey would walk on these garments as he bore Jesus toward the temple.

Someone raised a cry: "Hosanna! Hosanna to the Son of David!" (Matt. 21:9) The other spectators echoed the glad words. The Hebrew word meant, "Save, we pray." But it implied much more than that: the Messiah was coming!

The excited multitudes waved their palm fronds harder and shouted louder as the procession neared the temple gate. "Hosanna! Blessed is he who comes in the name of the Lord! Blessed is the coming kingdom of our Father David; Hosanna in the highest!" (Mark 11:9, 10)

The words became more open and frank as the people's hopes rose with their courage. "Blessed is he who comes in the name of the Lord, even the King of Israel!" (John 12:13)

Clearly, the people wanted Jesus to become their king and to cast off the Roman yoke.

When they reached the city, Jesus dismounted outside the gates and walked into the temple itself. The grounds covered 35 acres, and the polished white marble of the temple glistened so brightly that many considered it to be the most beautiful structure in the world. Herod had begun the temple about fifteen years before his death. The work was continuing, but was not yet complete when Jesus entered it on that fateful day.

Jesus walked along the eastern wall, which separated the temple from the Mount of Olives. This section had broad double columns of magnificent construction. It was a place for walking and talking, for admiring the grandeur of the structure erected to honor God—despite the fact that the despotic king Herod had erected it in imitation of the first temple constructed by King Solomon.

Jesus moved through an area which had a synagogue, sacrificial animal booths, and various shops, as well as moneychangers' tables, not far from the Great

Sanhedrin's meeting hall of hewn stone. But when Jesus entered the temple, instead of proclaiming himself the Messiah as the people had expected, he began to perform acts of righteous anger. In the Court of the Gentiles, under Solomon's Cloister, the teacher from Galilee overturned the tables of the moneychangers and the dove sellers. Jesus raised his voice so that all in the great courtyard could hear. *"Is it not written, 'My house shall be called a house of prayer for all the nations?' But you have made it a robbers' den!"* (Mark 12:17)

Jesus remained in the temple until the evening, and then left the city. But meanwhile the chief priests and scribes who had witnessed Jesus' actions began once again to plot against him, this time even more desperately. For they were now aware that if Jesus were not immediately destroyed, it would be impossible to move against him later.

That was a major turning point in the life of Jesus of Nazareth. The people had been surprised that he had not declared himself the Messiah. He hadn't behaved at all as they had expected. Even the disciples were perplexed.

But the religious leaders had no doubts at all what must be done. Jesus must be stopped, and quickly. It was just a matter of time until they accomplished their aims.

On Tuesday, two days after his entry into the temple, the elders and chief priests challenged his authority as he was teaching.

The leaders were afraid to seize Jesus because of his popularity with the people, so they attempted to entrap him by asking whether it was proper to pay taxes to the Romans. "Teacher," the spokesman said, framing his question in a way that made it seem innocent, "we know that you are truthful and teach the way of God in truth, and defer to no one, for you are not partial to any." (Matt. 22:16)

It was insincere flattery, intended to hide the pointed question which was to follow. The spokesman continued, "Tell us, therefore, what do you think? Is it lawful to give a poll-tax to Caesar, or not?" (Matt. 22:17)

The spectators stirred uneasily. Here, in this public place, Jesus' enemies had contrived a question which could get him into trouble with the authorities. For if Jesus answered that it was not lawful, the Romans would consider that he was inciting the people not to pay their taxes to the emperor.

But Jesus was aware that he was being tempted by a hypocritical question. Therefore, he demanded to be shown a coin; and when they brought him one, Jesus asked whose image was on it. The answer was obvious: "Caesar's." (Mark 12:16) The comment from Jesus was not at all obvious. It was a masterpiece of reasoning and diplomacy. *"Then render to Caesar the things that are Caesar's and to God the things that are God's!"* (Mark 12:17)

At the end of this day, as Jesus concluded his warning that people had a choice of heaven or eternal punishment, he walked apart with his disciples and spoke privately to them.

"You know that after two days the Passover is coming, and the Son of Man is to be delivered up for crucifixion." (Matt. 26:2)

It was true. At that moment, the chief priests and elders of the people were consulting in Caiaphas' court about how to seize Jesus by stealth and kill him. It was decided, however, not to seize him during Passover, as they were afraid that a riot would break out among the people.

Jesus crossed the Kidron Valley to another small village on the side of the Mount of Olives. That night, he was a guest of Simon the leper in Bethphage.

The Gospel of Saint Matthew indicates that it was during this night that Judas Iscariot approached the chief priests with a question: "What are you willing to give me to deliver him up to you?" (Matt. 26:15)

The delighted religious leaders offered the betrayer thirty pieces of silver. The money was accepted by Judas. Judas promised to turn Jesus over to them at an opportune moment when Jesus was apart from the people.

On Thursday, with the arrival of the Passover, Matthew declares that the disciples asked Jesus where he wanted them to prepare the Passover meal. Jesus told them that when they entered Jerusalem, a man carrying a pitcher of water would conduct them to the room where they were to celebrate Passover.

That evening, Jesus reclined at the table with the twelve. The disciples imitated him, leaning on their left hands to eat with their right. They sat on pillows before a low table on which was placed a large piece of unleavened bread, a cup, and a container of wine.

Jesus was solemn. He began by looking around the room and saying, *"I have earnestly desired to eat this Passover with you before I suffer, for I say to you, I shall never again eat it until it is fulfilled in the kingdom of God."* (Luke 22:15–16)

The disciples exchanged puzzled glances. First Jesus hadn't declared himself Messiah after the triumphal entry into Jerusalem four days before. Now he was talking about suffering as he had earlier, when he had three times told them he was going to Jerusalem to die. None of it made any sense to the twelve men.

Jesus took the traditional cup of Passover wine, gave thanks to God and passed it to the disciples. *"Take this,"* he said somberly, *"and share it among yourselves. For I say to you, I will not drink of the fruit of the vine from now on until the kingdom of heaven comes."* (Luke 22:17–18)

Jesus lifted the bread and broke it after giving thanks. He handed the pieces to his disciples with the words: *"This is my body which is given for you; do this in remembrance of me."* (Luke 22:19)

The terribly solemn meal was further darkened by Jesus' obvious distress of spirit. He looked over the men who had followed him for about three years and announced sadly, *"One of you will betray me."* (John 13:21)

A low murmur of surprise swept through the circle

of disciples. A general whisper of denial filled the room. Simon Peter, one of four fishermen who had left their nets to follow Jesus, gestured to John, son of Zebedee, who was the disciple closest to Jesus. Peter whispered to John to ask Jesus whom he meant.

John asked quietly, "Lord, who is it?" (John 13:25)

Jesus answered softly that the one to whom he gave the morsel of bread was his betrayer.

All the disciples leaned forward in anticipation as Jesus deliberately took a piece of the bread, slowly dipped it in the communal bowl, and then held it up. Every breath was held until Jesus extended the bread toward Judas.

Jesus said gently, quietly, *"What you do—do quickly."* (John 13:27)

The eleven other disciples frowned at each other as Judas Iscariot, the dripping morsel in his hand, sat uncomfortably. Then the disciples relaxed. Jesus was probably telling Judas to buy something needed for the feast, or maybe to give to the poor. After all, wasn't Judas Iscariot the little band's treasurer? Didn't he carry the common purse?

Judas immediately dropped the morsel onto the low table, shoved himself to his feet, and left the room. He went out into the quiet, moonlit night and walked toward a place where he knew the religious leaders would be waiting with temple guards.

When the Last Supper was finished, Jesus went across the Kidron Valley east of the city and entered a garden on the Mount of Olives. Every one of the disciples knew the place—including Judas Iscariot— for Jesus had often gone there before. Now he went, with a heavy heart, to a final session in the Garden of Gethsemane.

In the moonlit softness of the perfumed garden, Jesus drew aside Peter, James, and John. To the three men who had become closest to him, Jesus gave final instruction. *"My soul is deeply grieved, to the point of death; remain here and keep watch with me."* (Matt. 26:38)

Jesus made his way through the olive trees and fell on his face in prayer: *"My Father, if it is possible, let this cup pass from me."* (Matt. 26:39)

Then, having said what was deepest in his heart, Jesus added another sincere sentence. *"Yet not as I will, but as You will. Your will, Lord; not mine."* (Matt. 26:39)

Twice Jesus interrupted his anguished prayers to come back to the three disciples. They had gone to sleep. He upbraided them gently for sleeping when they should have been watching. Then Jesus returned to his solitary vigil of prayer.

Luke records a significant phrase: "And being in an agony, he was praying very fervently; and his sweat became like drops of blood falling down upon the ground." (Luke 22:44)

Finally, Jesus reached an inner peace; he was ready for what lay ahead. He was standing when Judas Iscariot returned with what John calls a Roman cohort (600 men), officers from the chief priests and Pharisees. They streamed across the Kidron Valley and poured into the garden on the Mount of Olives. Their flaming torches struck light from their weapons. The startled eleven disciples scrambled to their feet, all sleep vanishing from their eyes, as Judas stepped forward to mark the victim.

"Hail, Rabbi!" Judas said, lowering his eyes from Jesus' own. (Matt. 26:49) Judas kissed Jesus' bearded cheek and stepped back. (Mark 14:45)

The signal was recognized; the officers seized Jesus. He was led as a prisoner back to Jerusalem.

9

JESUS' TRIAL

The Gospel of Saint John records that after Jesus was betrayed by Judas, he was led before Annas, the titular high priest. Although Annas had not been high priest for some time, it was he who first interrogated Jesus that night about his teachings.

Jesus answered: *"I have spoken openly to the world; I always taught in the synagogue, and in the temple, where all the Jews come together; and I spoke nothing in secret. Why do you question me? Question those who have heard what I spoke to them about; behold, they know what I said."* (John 18:20–21)

At this, one of the soldiers standing near Jesus struck him, saying: "Is that the way you answer the high priest?" (John 18:22)

Jesus replied: *"If I have spoken wrongly, bear witness to the wrong; but if rightly, why do you strike me?"* (John 18:23)

Annas seemed to have had enough of the teacher from Galilee. The former high priest ordered Jesus sent in bonds to Caiaphas, Annas' son-in-law and the official high priest.

The second interrogation was apparently held very late on that Thursday night. The word had obvi-

In Search
of
Historic Jesus
†

Both New Testament and non-Gospel stories about Jesus are told in *In Search of Historic Jesus*. Here magi are depicted with Mary and Joseph and the infant Jesus.

A possible scientific explanation for the Star of Bethlehem is offered in this ancient cuneiform tablet from Babylonia.

Staatliche Museem, East Berlin

Although the Gospels are mostly silent about
Jesus' boyhood, it is assumed that he
learned the carpenter's trade from Joseph.

About eighteen years of Jesus' boyhood and young manhood are omitted from the Gospels. Legends, however, claim Jesus accompanied a caravan to India while he was a boy.

A legend claims Jesus visited Britain in company with Joseph of Arimathea. These Glastonbury ruins are said to stand where the boy Jesus once built a wattle church.

Jesus' baptism is reenacted here, with Utah's Jordan River substituting for the original river of the same name in Israel.

The New Testament indicates that Jesus of Nazareth
raised his friend Lazarus from the dead and set
off a controversy that led directly to his crucifixion.

Jesus is shown riding into
Jerusalem to the glad cries of
people who expected him to
announce he was the Jews'
long awaited Messiah.

According to the Gospels, Jesus celebrated a unique
meal with bread and wine, now known as the Last
Supper, during his last time together with the apostles.
A short time later, he was betrayed and crucified.

Judas Iscariot approaches Jesus in the Garden of
Gethsemane to betray him with a kiss, while officials
wait to seize the Nazarene teacher for trial.

According to the Gospels, Jesus of Nazareth
was illegally tried at night, in violation of Jewish laws.

Although the Gospels say Jesus of Nazareth was forced to carry his own cross part of the way to the place of his execution, research has disclosed that condemned victims carried only the crossbeam, or patibulum, and not the entire cross.

A Roman soldier nails Jesus' feet to the upright portion of the cross.

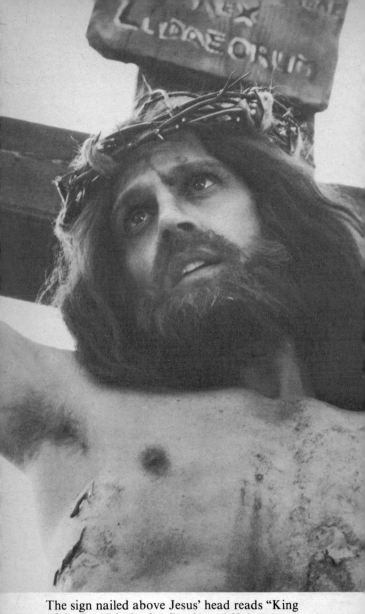

The sign nailed above Jesus' head reads "King of the Jews" in Latin, Greek, and Hebrew.

Joseph of Arimethea and Nicodemus were forced
to make hasty and incomplete burial
arrangements for the crucified Jesus because by Jewish
law burial had to be completed before the
sunset beginning the Sabbath.

One of the most intriguing mysteries of all time is still
unanswered by modern scientists studying the
Shroud of Turin: how did the figure of a crucified man,
matching the details of the Gospels, get on the cloth?

One of the strangest myths common to Indians of
North, Central, and South America is that of a bearded
white god who appeared to their ancestors at
about the time Jesus was crucified on another continent.

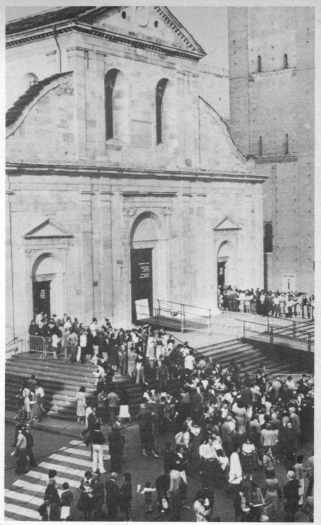

A rare public exhibition of the Shroud of Turin drew
more than three million people to the
Cathedral of St. John the Baptist in Turin, Italy,
during the summer of 1978.

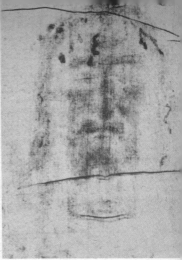

Modern scientists have determined that the image on the Shroud of Turin cannot be a painting but are unable to explain how the positive image (right) and negative views of the head and full body were made.

The New Testament explains how Jesus healed a man at the Pool of Bethesda, which had five porches, or porticos. Scientific digging has confirmed not only the existence of the site but of the porticos as well.

William Holdman

"Gordon's Calvary," said to resemble a skull, is one site suspected of being the Golgotha, or Calvary, of the New Testament. The words Calvary and Golgotha both mean skull or place of a skull.

Don O. Thorpe

The "Garden Tomb" is adjacent to "Gordon's Calvary" in Jerusalem and is regarded by some researchers as a logical site for Jesus' burial. Tombs carved out of limestone and sealed by a rolling stone set in a trough were common in Jesus' time.

Don O. Thorpe

Another possible site for Jesus' tomb is the
Church of the Holy Sepulchre in Jerusalem. Roman
Catholics generally believe this
to be the place where Jesus was buried.

William Holdman

No original copies of the Bible manuscripts are
known to exist, but fragments found in Egypt have
been dated about a century and a half after Jesus'
lifetime. These fragments are from the New
Testament Gospel of John.

John Rylands Library, Manchester, England

ously already been spread about Jesus' capture, for Matthew declares that the scribes and elders were gathered together. He is joined by Mark and John in saying that this meeting was held in the high priest's home. (Matt. 26:58; Mark 14:53; John 18:15) Luke also agrees, but says that "when it was day, the council of elders of the people assembled, both high priests and scribes, and they led him away to their council chamber." (Luke 22:6)

The palace of Caiaphas is usually considered the place where Jesus was heard by the Sanhedrin. Peter had run away with the other apostles when Jesus was taken prisoner in the Garden of Gethsemane, but he returned and entered the courtyard, warming himself by a fire. Servants and slaves looked at him curiously, discerning the accent of a Galilean. Before the rooster crowed that morning, Peter three times denied knowing Jesus.

Inside Caiaphas' home, the council members listened to a parade of witnesses. They falsely accused Jesus of various crimes in an effort to secure the death penalty. But the witnesses couldn't agree on Jesus' alleged crimes.

Jesus heard his accusers in silence, not deigning to answer them.

The question arises as to who was present at this illegal late-night religious tribunal where a predetermined verdict had already been decided.

Joseph of Arimathea apparently took no part in Jesus' condemnation; nor did he do anything about it. He either abstained from the voting or was absent from the meeting itself. The Gospels don't mention Joseph of Arimathea at all in this context, though they later indicate he had not consented to Jesus' death. Months before, Nicodemus had made a cautious defense of Jesus. (John 7:50–53) It is not clear from the Gospels whether Nicodemus spoke for Jesus again. If Nicodemus was present at the illegal night meeting, the Gospels don't say. Neither do they say he was absent. However, in our reconstruction of the scene, both

Nicodemus and Joseph of Arimathea are in the kangaroo court.

Joseph rose to speak. "Why is he bound? There has been no judgment passed against him."

The rich merchant moved forward as though to free Jesus' bonds, but Caiaphas motioned to the temple guards, who wordlessly blocked Joseph's actions by crossing their staves in front of him.

Nicodemus also rose, but with care. "These witnesses have not even agreed among themselves, but they haven't been properly coached, which surprises me in view of all these illegal activities!"

"We have not called all the witnesses," the high priest reminded the two council members. "But we shall hear them now."

Two witnesses with shifty eyes, who had been heavily bribed, came forward. Their accusation was that Jesus had said that he was able to destroy the temple and rebuild it in three days. (Matt. 26:61) The council members nodded with satisfaction. That was more like it! Those witnesses knew what to say!

Joseph of Arimathea and Nicodemus knew that was not what Jesus had said. But it didn't matter; the decision of the tribunal had been set beforehand on a death penalty. All the high priest had to do was to keep the trial on course.

"Three days?" Caiaphas frowned. "Isn't the prisoner also claimed to have said something to the effect that if he was killed, he would rise again the third day?"

Jesus had said to the disciples near Capernaum: "The Son of Man is to be delivered up into the hands of men, and they will kill him; and when he has been killed, he will rise again three days later." (Mark 9:31)

The disciples had been afraid to ask Jesus to explain the remark, which they hadn't understood. Now the Jewish leaders knew about Jesus' claim.

Caiaphas stood up from his ornate chair and faced Jesus. "Do you make no answer? What is it that these men are testifying against you?" (Matt. 26:62) Caia-

phas waved his hand toward the last two witnesses.
Again Jesus kept silent.

The high priest pursed his lips and stroked his
beard. He wanted the witness to incriminate himself.
That would be better than all these witnesses. Caiaphas
pointed a long finger at the prisoner and spoke emphati-
cally. "I charge you under oath—by the living God—
that you tell us whether you are the Christ." (Matt.
26:63)

Jesus raised his voice so all might hear. *"You have
said it yourself; nevertheless I tell you, hereafter you
shall see the Son of Man sitting at the right hand of
Power, and coming on the clouds of heaven."* (Matt.
26:64)

That was what the high priest was waiting for!
The prisoner had played directly into Caiaphas' hands.
He tore his robes in the traditional rite of hearing
blasphemy and cried loudly to the assembled elders.

"He has blasphemed! Why do we need further witnesses?" (Matt. 26:65)

The elders became a mob. In righteous religious
indignation, they turned their rage and frustration at
Jesus. He had openly challenged them in debate, pub-
licly called them hypocrites, as well as other unsavory
names, and contradicted their doctrines. Now, in one
sentence, he had condemned himself!

Caiaphas shouted over the tumult: "What do you
think?" They answered, "He is deserving of death!"
(Matt. 26:66)

They surged forward, maddened by the lust for
vengeance, and began to spit in Jesus' face. They beat
him with their fists. Some slapped him.

Out of the surging human sea of hatred, resent-
ment and physical violence, someone called to Jesus:
"Prophesy to us, you Christ; who hit you?" (Matt. 26:
68)

Jesus' final ordeal had begun.

When morning came, the chief priests and elders
worked out their plan to put Jesus to death. They had
illegally met and condemned him, but it would take the

Roman governor's pronouncement of death to have Jesus killed.

Pontius Pilate would never order anyone to be put to death because of a religious matter; it would have to be a civil or military threat to prompt the Judean procurator to order the death sentence.

Jesus was handed over to the red-clad Roman soldiers, who took him through the gate and into the praetorium while the religious leaders waited outside. If they entered the praetorium, they would become ritually unclean and could not eat the Passover meal. (John 18:28) So Jesus was held in the forbidden place which was called *Gabbatha* in Aramaic. The Greek word was *lithostroton,* which translates as "stone pavement."

There was disagreement among scholars about where it was, but archaeologists have recently unearthed a huge stone parade ground near the Tower of Antonia, which was next to the outer temple court. The governor had his judgment seat there. He could also review his cavalry, for the courtyard was large enough to be a parade ground. Some Roman game had been scratched into the stones. The lines for the game were deep enough to survive 2,000 years.

The praetorium had originally been a military headquarters. In Pilate's time, the word had come to signify the governor's headquarters building or official residence. Pilate used the praetorium when he was in Jerusalem, although he usually lived at Caesarea, by the cool shores of the Mediterranean.

Pontius Pilate walked angrily from this forbidden area and through the gate to where the agitated religious leaders were waiting. He was irritated at being summoned from his bed at so late an hour. The governor demanded: "What charges are you bringing against this man?" (John 18:29)

The religious leaders shouted back: "If this man were not an evil doer, we would not have delivered him to you!" (John 18:30)

Pilate was not in the mood for such responses. He snapped: "Take him yourselves, and judge him according to your law!"

· The chief priests responded: "We are not permitted to put anyone to death!" (John 18:31)

Although this was true, it made no impression on the governor. However, before he could turn away and leave the accusers more frustrated, someone shouted a key charge of insurrection.

"We found this man misleading our nation and forbidding people to pay taxes to Caesar, and saying that he himself is Christ, a king." (Luke 23:2)

That stopped the governor. He'd had enough trouble with the rebellious Jews since he had been made procurator. Usually they gave him trouble over religious matters. Once they had objected because he had brought standards into the city. These were not flags, but Roman insignia on staves, with representations of eagles. Reproduction of any kind of image was reprehensible to the Jews, whose faceless, invisible God had forbidden making images of man or beast. In the end, Pilate had given in; the Jews' willingness to die in a riot for their strange beliefs had caused the offensive standards to be removed.

Another time, Pilate had actually placed his troops' naked swords against the obstinate Jews' throats, but they had obviously been willing to accept death rather than yield where religion was concerned. Again, Pilate had given in. Another time, he had used temple funds to build an aqueduct to bring water to Jerusalem. The Jews had objected again, and Pilate had faced a riot.

He didn't want another uprising; procurators could be replaced by Rome, just as the ethnarch Archelaus had been years before. No, Pilate admitted to himself, he didn't dare have another riot reported to the emperor. Insurrection? That was a military matter.

Pilate reentered the praetorium and faced Jesus.

He had been a prisoner several hours. His beard and face were streaked with white lines where perspiration had dried. His face and parts of his upper body were turning blue or black and swelling from the blows he had received. Still, the prisoner stood serenely, as one who has an inner strength or conviction not evident to observers.

Pilate pursed his lips at this calm figure who stood in bonds before him. "Are you the king of the Jews?" (Luke 22:3)

Jesus replied, *"Are you saying this on your own initiative, or did others tell you about me?"* (John 18:34)

The governor was astonished. "Am I a Jew? Your own nation and the chief priests delivered you to me!" Jesus didn't reply, so Pilate demanded: "What have you done?" (John 18:35)

Jesus replied: *"My kingdom is not of this world. If my kingdom were of this world, then my servants would be fighting, that I might not be delivered to the Jews. But as it is my kingdom is not of this realm."* (John 18:36)

Pilate pursued his question, trying to make sense of the strange responses of the prisoner. "You are a king?" (John 18:37)

Jesus answered: *"You say correctly that I am a king. For this I have been born, and for this I have come into the world, to bear witness to the truth. Everyone who is of the truth hears my voice."* (John 18:37)

The governor shrugged and said to Jesus: "What is truth?" (John 18:38) Then he sighed and turned away from the sweaty, bleeding, and battered prisoner, returning to the waiting Jewish leaders outside the praetorium. "I find no guilt in this man," the governor announced. (Luke 23:4)

The chief priests and the crowd they had gathered refused to give up. They insisted: "He stirs up the people, teaching them all over Judea, starting from Galilee, even as far as this place!" (Luke 23:5)

Pilate's eyes narrowed thoughtfully. He then asked whether Jesus was a Galilean; and when told that he was, Pilate sent him to Herod who had jurisdiction over Galilee.

The chief priests and scribes followed Jesus and his escort to Herod's fortified palace on the city's western wall. Herod's soldiers were dressed in blue tunics. They received the battered prisoner from the red-clad Roman soldiers and took Jesus to Herod Antipas.

The tetrarch of Galilee was glad when he saw the Nazarene. For a long time, as Luke explains, Herod Antipas had been hearing about Jesus. The man who had ordered John the Baptist beheaded hoped to see Jesus perform some miracle or sign.

The ruler of Galilee began questioning Jesus. The prisoner did not reply. Herod's temper began to rise. His voice rose as he continued asking Jesus questions, but the teacher of Galilee stood in silence.

The chief priests and scribes began accusing Jesus in loud voices. The more vehement they became, the less responsive Jesus was to the tetrarch's questions, and the angrier Herod Antipas grew.

Finally, he had enough. Herod Antipas turned to his soldiers. The Galilean ruler's lip curled in scorn. Herod Antipas jerked his head toward Jesus. The troops understood.

In a moment, blue tunics surrounded Jesus. They mocked him and treated him with contempt. Then they dressed Jesus in a gorgeous robe and sent him back to Pilate. (Luke 23:11)

Pilate was trapped. He had his unwelcome prisoner back again. The governor called the Jewish rulers and summed up the situation.

"You brought this man to me as one who incites the people to rebellion. But, having examined him before you, I have found no guilt in this man regarding the charges which you make against him." (Luke 23:14)

A roar of disappointment cut him off, but Pilate was not governor of a troublesome district because he was easily intimidated. He held up his hands and shouted as though he had not been interrupted.

"No, nor has Herod, for he sent him back to us; and behold, nothing deserving death has been done by him." (Luke 23:15)

Again, the mob's angry cries arose, but Pilate was firm. He called out his decision. "I will therefore chastise him and release him." (Luke 23:16)

Pilate turned to reenter the praetorium, but the roar of disapproval stopped him. He turned, undecided, afraid that a riot might be imminent. Was there some way to compromise?

Pilate suddenly had an idea. He held up his hands again and called out. "You have a custom that I release someone for you at the Passover. Do you want me to release the King of the Jews?" (John 18:39)

The crowd answered: "No! Don't release this man! Give us Barabbas!" (John 18:40)

It wasn't an answer Pilate had expected.

Barabbas was a robber, murderer, and insurrectionist. He was a political prisoner because of his civil resistance to the military authorities. Logically, the people should have chosen Jesus over such a character. But they had chosen, and Pilate was suddenly in a tighter spot than he had thought possible a few minutes ago. The worst part of it was that he knew the demonstrators were having Jesus held because they were envious of his power and popularity with the people.

But Pilate was afraid that if he had Jesus released against the will of the religious leaders, he would risk another riot and possible recall by the emperor. So he continued to try to work something out with Jesus' accusers.

Pilate raised his voice. "What shall I do with Jesus who is called Christ?" (Matt. 27:22)

The mob had been prepared for that question. They shouted as one man: "Let him be crucified!" (Matt. 27:23)

The procurator was astonished at the severity of the request. Jews never crucified people. That was a very old practice of several other nations. Herodotus, the famous Greek historian, has recorded the Persians practiced this cruel form of death six centuries before Christ. The indescribably protracted anguish of this form of death had also been known to the Carthaginians, the Assyrians, the Germans, and others. The Romans had been among the last to practice crucifixion, and the practice would continue until 315 AD when it was finally abolished by the emperor Constantine.

Usually, however, the Romans only crucified slaves and insurrectionists. It was the lowest form of death and especially abhorrent to the Jews, whose ancient laws declared that anyone who hung on a tree was accursed of God.

But Pilate had no choice now. The accusers were chanting loudly and violently: "Crucify him! Crucify! Crucify! Crucify!"

Pilate saw that he was accomplishing nothing. Instead, a riot was starting. He couldn't afford that. He called for a basin of water, washed his hands symbolically in front of the screaming, senseless mob, and called out: "I am innocent of this man's blood! See to it yourselves!" (Matt. 27:24)

Pilate was beaten. He released Barabbas, and ordered Jesus scourged prior to crucifixion—a standard Roman practice.

Jesus' trial was over.

The religious leaders had won.

In the early morning hours of a Friday on a spring day in Jerusalem, Jesus was on his way to death.

10

THE ROAD TO CALVARY

Jesus was to be executed by the Roman soldiers. These were the world's finest fighting men. The Romans were not squeamish about killing other human beings. These soldiers, who had conquered most of the known world, were ingenious when it came to killing civilians —especially Jews. Since a thousand or more civilians might be crucified as the result of a single incident, the Roman troops were sometimes sadistically inventive in the manner in which they carried out an already sadistic execution. A recent excavation disclosed a victim of the cross who had been nailed through the heels and between the two bones of the forearm. The Roman soldiers' diversion was to find new and innovative ways to take a life by crucifixion.

Such things may have been appealing to the legionnaires who had accompanied their governor from his coastal headquarters at Caesarea to Jerusalem. Pilate regularly made the 65-mile journey at major festivals, such as the Passover, because it was at these times that the Jews were most likely to cause a disturbance. They could never seem to get it through their heads that they were a conquered people. Sometimes the soldiers had broken their traditional peacetime boredom by cracking a few Jewish heads when they resisted Pilate. Sometimes the legionnaires got to chase a Zealot—a member of a nationalist political party created shortly after the death of King Herod. But the Zealots operated singly, hiding daggers beneath their cloaks with which to suddenly slash a solitary soldier or a Hellenized Jew. Then these *sicarii,* as the Romans called the daggermen, would slip away in the crowds. The soldiers preferred other kinds of diversion, such as the prospect now before them: crucifying someone called "King of the Jews."

Jesus, bloody and bruised from the blows he had received at the hands of the Sanhedrin members, was now seized by the Roman soldiers attached to Pilate and stripped of his robe. The soldiers then dressed him in a purple robe and put a crown of thorns on his head. (Mark 15:17; John 19:2)

The mocking significance of the purple robe and the crown of thorns has to do with the fact that purple was the color of royalty in the ancient world, while the laurel wreath was traditionally given to conquering heroes, athletes, and poets. Thus, bowing in mockery before Jesus, the soldiers cried: "Hail, King of the Jews!" (Matt. 27:30)

But that was too passive for violent men. They began to spit on their victim in the age-old expression of utter disdain. Then the soldiers scourged Jesus.

The Scriptures give no details of this whipping which the Romans always inflicted upon a crucifixion victim. But archaeological and other studies have shown that this punishment involved a whip made of 18-inch handles with three or more leather cords or thongs. These were made more vicious by inserting sheep knuckles or sharp metal objects into the tip. When the cords struck, they gouged out chunks of flesh.

The Jews had a law that no man might be struck more than 40 times. Traditionally, only 39 stripes were administered. But the Romans had no such restrictions. They stripped their victim, tied him to a post, and then flagellated him. A soldier stood on either side of the victim and took turns striking with their whistling whips.

Each blow, struck alternately right to left, methodically covered the victim from neck to ankles. As many as a hundred and twenty blows landed, jerked clear with the pieces of quivering flesh, and then slashed down again and again. A man could die under such merciless lashes.

The bloody body was made more painful by pulling the victim's robe back over his gaping wounds. The serum and blood dried, adhering to the robe, so that each step or movement which tore open a wound added to the pain.

But at least Jewish scourging victims got to have their clothes back; the Romans honored this yearning for modesty and did not run the victims naked through the streets to the cross, as they did with non-Jews, according to Josephus.

When the soldiers had finished their preliminary torture, Jesus was led off to be crucified.

He was not to die alone. Two other prisoners were brought out of the dungeons and driven through the streets of Jerusalem by the Roman soldiers. According to tradition, the criminals were named Dismas (or Dysmas) and Gestas. They are variously described as thieves, robbers, or malefactors.

The three crucifixion victims were burdened with their own crossbeam, called a *patibulum*. This was the shorter, horizontal bar of the cross. Each *patibulum* weighed about 80 pounds and was of olive wood.

Jesus was already weakened from his anguished ordeal in the garden and the various blows struck before the whipping. The shock to the body, plus the loss of blood, made Jesus stagger and fall under his load. Tradition says he fell three times on the way to the crucifixion.

As the three condemned men were led through the streets, a Cyrenian named Simon was told to carry Jesus' cross. (Matt. 27:32; Mark 15:21; Luke 23:26) Since Cyrene was a North African country, it has been assumed that Simon was a black man. Other sources suggest he was a Jew from that country who had come to the Passover. Whoever he was, Simon the Cyrenian was suddenly pressed into service. He joined the procession of the condemned, carrying Jesus' cross to the execution site.

The place was called Golgotha in Hebrew (John 19:17) and Calvary in Latin. The word means "skull" or "place of the skulls." By tradition, it was on a hill. It was outside the city, near a road, and probably northwest of Jerusalem.

A great multitude followed Jesus to his death. Many of them were women, mourning and lamenting. (Luke 23:27)

Jesus turned to them and spoke through lips swollen with the blows he had received over the last several hours:

> Daughters of Jerusalem, stop weeping for me, but weep for yourselves and for your children.
>
> For the day is coming when they will say, 'Blessed are the barren, and the wombs that never bore, and the breasts that never nursed.'
>
> Then they will begin to say to the mountains, 'Fall on us,' and to the hills, 'cover us.'
>
> For if they do these things in the green tree, what will happen to the dry? (Luke 23:28–31)

The mournful procession reached Calvary. The Gospels are mercifully silent on the procedure for what happened next, simply declaring, "There they crucified him and the criminals, one on the right hand, the other on the left." (Luke 23:33)

Research suggests the details omitted by the Scriptures.

The three victims were forced to lie down on their backs. They were stripped to their loincloths and their shoulders were stretched onto the crossbeams. The soldiers pulled their victims' arms out full length along the rough beams. Roman nails, about five inches long, were held in place at the wrists or the base of the palms. The heavy wooden mallets rose and fell. The nails shot through the flesh and into the solid beam.

The screams and moans of the thieves were echoed in the anguished keening of the women who had followed Jesus from the city.

Jesus suffered the same fate; both hands were nailed to the cross. Then one spike was driven through both feet which had been placed one on top of the other so only a single nail was needed.

The squirming men, thrashing about in the agony which came from the pierced hands and feet, plus the destruction of intensely sensitive wrist nerves, were ready to be lifted up.

Jesus had prophesied being lifted onto the cross, although at the time it hadn't been understood. When he was talking to Nicodemus at night, Jesus had explained: "And as Moses lifted up the serpent in the wilderness, even so must the Son of Man be lifted up; that whoever believes may in him have eternal life." (John 3:14–15)

The reference was to Moses' experience with the people whom he had led out of Egypt. The freed Hebrew slaves had gone from the Red Sea toward Edom when they became impatient. They had no food or water and complained that Moses had brought them out of Egypt only to die in the desert. God sent "fiery serpents" who bit the people, so many died. When the people confessed their sins to Moses, the Lord had Moses make a bronze serpent and set it upon a standard. The bite victims who looked upon the symbol lived. (Numb. 21:4–9)

Jesus often referred to himself as the "Son of Man," a term used by the Prophet Ezekiel in the Old Testament.

Now, as Jesus had prophesied, he was to be lifted up.

The Romans had already placed the upright posts in the ground. The crossbeam with the suffering body of Jesus was lifted by legionnaires. The *patibulum* was slid upward along the sturdy vertical post until the soldiers' arms could reach no further. Then they used their spears to shove the ends of the crossbeam up until it slid into a notch cut into the upright post. A couple of quick blows by the Roman mallets and great spikes slipped into pre-existing holes. The crossbeam was locked in place on the upright post.

The force of gravity would pull the arms of those crucified down about 65 degrees. The pain was excruciating. The lungs filled with air, but it was impossible to exhale without relieving the pull on the chest. The only way to do this was to push against the foot nail and pull upward with the bicep muscles. However, the gravity pull would then make the arms sag again. Eventually, asphyxiation would set in. In a few moments, a blue tinge from the lack of oxygen would spread over the entire torso, above and below the loincloth.

The Gospels record that the soldiers offered Jesus the traditional drugged wine. It didn't entirely kill the pain of the cross; nothing could do that. But it helped.

The soldiers turned to Jesus' possessions. The dice rattled as the soldiers threw them to decide who would possess the garments of the so-called King of the Jews.

Pilate, angered at the way the Jewish religious leaders had forced him to have Jesus crucified, had ordered a sign prepared in three languages—Hebrew, Greek, and Latin. A soldier brought it, placed a ladder against the back of Jesus' cross, climbed up, and reached over the top part of the upright to pound the sign into place above Jesus' head.

It read: "JESUS OF NAZARETH, THE KING OF THE JEWS." (John 19:19)

Pilate was not mocking Jesus as the soldiers had. For, as John records, when the chief priests had read the sign, they told Pilate that instead of writing "the King of the Jews," he should have written that this is what Jesus called himself. But Pilate answered: "What I have written I have written." (John 19:21–22)

The soldiers finished their gambling and sat down to watch and wait. Fortunately, these were Jews who couldn't be allowed the normal several days to die on the cross over the Sabbath, so their deaths would be hastened later that day. About midafternoon, a soldier with a heavy mallet would methodically break each victim's legs. With this support gone, all the man's weight was thrown onto his shoulders, already nearly torn from their sockets. The man would be unable to exhale the poisoned air from his lungs. Death would come more quickly, but with the added horror and pain of broken bones, incredible muscle spasms, and lack of oxygen.

But in the meantime, the people passing by the road wagged their heads in mockery and called up to Jesus. "You who would destroy the temple and rebuild it in three days—save yourself!"

Another scoffer called: "Yes! If you are the Son of God, come down from the cross!"

The chief priests and scribes who had come to mock Jesus joined the elders in shouting cruel remarks.

"He saved others; he cannot save himself."

"If he really is the king of Israel, let him now come down from the cross and we'll believe in him."

"He trusts in God, let Him deliver him now."

"That's right! If God takes pleasure in him, let it be, for this Jesus has said, 'I am the Son of God.'" (Matt. 27:39–43)

Even the two criminals ignored their own agony to speak to Jesus who was hanging between them. The one traditionally called Gestas painfully thrust his body upward with the nailed feet so he could hurl a challenge at Jesus: "Are you not the Christ? Save yourself and us!"

But the other criminal, traditionally called Dismas, rebuked him: "Don't you even fear God, since you're under the same sentence of condemnation?" Then he said to Jesus: "Lord, remember me when you come to your kingdom."

Jesus replied, *"Truly I say to you, today you shall be with me in Paradise."* (Luke 23:39–43)

Nearly three hours had passed since the crucifixion had begun. The waiting continued. Each of the four soldiers had claimed his winnings. They had divided the garments into four parts so each would win something. The luckiest man had won Jesus' tunic. Another had won the garment worn next to the skin, which the Greeks called a *khiton*. (John 19:32)

The crowd's hostility waned during the prolonged suffering, and they drifted away. The women who had followed Jesus eased toward the cross.

Jesus opened his eyes and recognized his mother, his aunt, Mary Magdalene, and several others. But Jesus' eyes centered on his mother's tear-streaked face and on his disciple, John, who stood beside her.

Jesus pulled himself with great difficulty to the point where he could exhale the stale air which was poisoning his body. *"Woman,"* he said to his mother, *"behold your son!"* Then, before his arms sagged again, he uttered a few words to the disciple: *"Behold your mother!"* (John 19:26–27)

John, son of Zebedee, understood that he was to take Mary, the mother of Jesus, into his own household.

Suddenly, about noon, the sky turned black. It was not a storm, for the rainy season was over. The spectators at the cross looked up apprehensively as the sun was obscured.

Was it an eclipse? Clouds? The Scriptures don't say. But the fast-moving darkness at noon engulfed the entire land for three hours. (Mark 15:33)

Crucifixion caused extreme thirst. In the agony of six hours of suffering, the demand for liquid became so intense in the dying Jesus that he finally voiced his need.

One of the soldiers plunged a staff's point into a sponge and then dipped it into a jar of sour wine. The Roman raised the dripping sponge above his head to where Jesus' mouth was, some nine feet off the ground.

After drinking a little of the liquid, Jesus turned his face away, saying softly, *"It is finished!"* (John 19:30)

At three o'clock, or the ninth hour of the Jewish day, Jesus startled the waiting people by crying out in a surprisingly loud voice: *"Eloi, eloi, lama sabach-thani?"* This was Aramaic for: *"My God, my God! Why have You forsaken me?"* (Mark 15:34)

Some of the bystanders thought that he was calling for Elijah. One man ran to fill the sponge with sour wine, and thrust it upward on a stick, saying, "Let us see if Elijah will come to take him down." (Mark 15: 35–36)

According to the Scriptures, Elijah had never died. Instead, he had been brought up to heaven in a whirl-wind and a fiery chariot. Many believed that he would come again at the time of the Messiah.

Jesus' last words on the cross, according to Luke, were: *"Father, into Your hands I commit my spirit!"* (Luke 24:46)

In that instant, an earthquake struck the area. In-side the city walls, the blue veil of the temple was torn in two. It was a symbolic rendering of the division which had long separated God from men.

At the cross, the centurion who had been in charge of the execution steadied himself against the earth's trembling and the sound of splitting rocks. He was frightened as he called out: "Truly this was the Son of God!" (Matt. 27:54)

This was a strange thing for a pagan Roman to say! But stranger things were to follow, for the soldier began praising God and exclaiming, "Certainly this man was innocent!" (Luke 23:47)

The watching multitudes who had come to see a brutal, cruel spectacle began beating their breasts in the Jewish manner of lamentation. They turned toward Jerusalem, their grief and remorse filling the air above the still, silent form on the center cross.

Nearby, their faces hidden in shawls or upturned in sadness marked by many tears, the women who had followed Jesus from Galilee stared in numb suffering.

In the gloom of that midafternoon darkness, Jesus of Nazareth sagged on the cross of Calvary.

Jesus was dead. The hopes of many people died with him.

But there was nothing they could do, except hastily

bury him before the sunset heralded the start of the Sabbath and the Passover when no work could be done—not even burying the dead.

But the body of a criminal, crucified on a Roman cross, was not usually allowed a decent burial. Unless it was ransomed, it rotted on the cross or was thrown into a common grave.

If anyone was to claim the body of Jesus and give it a proper burial, it would have to be someone with courage, authority, and an idea of where to bury the corpse.

The only person who met those qualifications was Joseph of Arimathea. He hurried toward the Antonia fortress to seek an audience with Pontius Pilate.

11

THE BURIAL
AND RESURRECTION
OF JESUS

The Gospel of Saint John explains that Joseph of Arimathea was a secret disciple of Jesus because he feared the Jews. (John 19:38) Each of the Synoptic Gospels adds a clue to the identity of this man, who had not been introduced in any of the four Gospels before the crucifixion. Joseph was rich and a pious member of the Sanhedrin. He had been waiting for the kingdom of God. Mark explains that Joseph of Arimathea now "gathered up courage and went in before Pilate" to ask for Jesus' body. (Mark 15:43)

Joseph could not enter the praetorium without defiling himself, so Pontius Pilate came out into the open courtyard to meet his visitor. Briefly, quietly, Joseph explained that it was the day of preparation for the Sabbath and that the bodies could not remain on the cross on the Sabbath, which was also a high holy day. Therefore, Joseph asked permission to take Jesus' body and bury it. (John 19:31)

What follows is a fictional recreation of the meeting between Pilate and Joseph of Arimathea.

* * *

Pilate decided to be lenient. "The Jews have already been here to ask that the victims' legs be broken. As soon as this Jesus is dead, you may have his body."

Joseph lowered his head and said quietly, "He is already dead, governor."

Pilate blinked in surprise. "Already dead? But that's impossible! They haven't had time to die since I gave permission to break the prisoners' legs!" "Nevertheless," Joseph replied softly, "Jesus of Nazareth is dead."

The Roman shook his head. "I have to marvel that such a thing has happened, Joseph. I'm sure you won't mind if I call a soldier and verify that?"

"Of course not, governor." (John 19:31–38; Matthew 27:14)

The governor's personal bodyguard summoned a centurion. He assured Pilate that he would personally check out the reported death. The officer marched briskly away from the open courtyard where Pilate had met the merchant in deference to his religious beliefs.

The governor glanced at the strange sky and asked about the darkness. "What do you make of it, Joseph?"

"I can't say, governor."

"Have you ever seen anything like it, Joseph?"

"Never."

"Neither have I. I don't know if it was an eclipse of the sun or a fast-moving storm, or what. Strange. Very strange! And the wild rumors which have been going around this city since then! You know, Joseph, I actually heard that some Jews claim that the blue veil in your temple was torn. I've heard that some dead people were known to have come out of their graves and were seen walking around." Pilate laughed nervously. "Weird things are told when something unusual happens in the sky, like today. Don't you agree?"

"Many things are hard to explain, governor." (Matthew 27:45; 27:51; 27:52)

There was an awkward silence while Pilate stared off toward the area where Jesus had been crucified. "Tell me, Joseph," the governor said abruptly, breaking the silence, "is it true that you are considered an honorable counselor of your people?" (Mark 15:43)

"I try to be."

"I also hear you are a good man, Joseph." (Luke 23:50)

"I would like to be thought so."

"And you are rich; everyone knows that." (Matthew 27:57)

Joseph lowered his eyes.

Pilate stroked his smooth chin, which was shaved in the Roman fashion, in contrast to the bearded appearance of the people over whom he ruled. Abruptly, having made a decision, Pilate gestured toward his visitor.

"Tell me, my rich friend, why is it a man like you begs the body of a crucified man?"

Joseph pursed his lips and thought a moment. But before he could frame an answer, Pilate pointed a long forefinger and exclaimed, "I have it! You're a disciple of that man from Galilee!"

Joseph nodded slightly. "I have been waiting for the kingdom of God." (Luke 23:51)

"But why you?" Pilate puzzled. "Rich. A member of the Sanhedrin. Respected . . ."

"And one who has read the Scriptures for years about the coming Messiah, Pilate, and one who is convinced that this Jesus of Nazareth *is* what we've been looking for all these centuries."

"Your friends on the council are not going to like having you talk that way, Joseph!"

The centurion returned, saluting briskly. "The criminal, Jesus of Nazareth, is dead, sir!"

Pilate marveled. "So soon? Are you sure?"

"Yes, sir! I personally saw the lance thrust into his side."

"Ah, yes!" Pilate said. He turned to Joseph. "Just a simple Roman precaution, you understand; a single expert stroke to make sure the victim is dead."

The centurion cleared his throat. Pilate frowned. "You have something else to report, centurion?"

"Yes, sir. That is, uh, sir . . ."

"Well?" the governor snapped.

"Sir, I have seen many such lance thrusts. But never have I seen what I saw just a few minutes ago."

Pilate was mildly curious. "What was that?"

"Well, sir, there came out blood and water." (John 19:34)

"Blood and water? From a lance thrust?"

"Yes, sir. I'm sure that's what it was. And one of the disciples was there—I don't know his name . . ."

"John," said Joseph. "His name is John, son of Zebedee."

"Yes, sir. Well, he also saw it. The blood and water."

Pilate shook his head. "The city is full of strange events today, centurion. Thank you for your report. I have given my friend here permission to take the body of the one they call Jesus."

Joseph of Arimathea thanked Pilate and went out with the soldier. But on the way to the execution site, Joseph stopped at a merchant's stall, looked over a display of linen, and bought a burial cloth.

Then Joseph made his way painfully back to the place where Jesus and the two thieves had been crucified. As he stood at the foot of the cross, Nicodemus arrived with a pack burro.

"Ah, Joseph, my friend! How sad the occasion that brings us both here at this time."

Joseph nodded. "I have bought a burial cloth, and I see that you brought spices." (John 19:39)

Nicodemus pointed to the packages lashed to either side of the small animal's sturdy back. "A hundred pounds of aloes and myrrh."

Joseph nodded in approval. "We shall have to hurry, Nicodemus."

Both men glanced apprehensively at the western sky and hastened to have the body removed from the cross.

The burial ritual of the Jews involved washing and anointing the body, placing the myrrh and aloes alongside the torso, and then drawing the burial cloth over the deceased. A chinstrap was placed around the head and lower jaw to hold it in place. Shards or small coins sometimes were placed on the eyelids.

It was all done very quickly, for the two men were in a hurry to finish before the sun went down. The task was made all the more difficult because rigor mortis set in more quickly in the body of a crucified man than in one who had died under normal circumstances.

But it was finally done. The body was wrapped from head to toe in a single long sheet.

"We've done all we can, Joseph," said Nicodemus.

The rich merchant nodded, sighed briefly, and glanced quickly over the shrouded figure. The legs were straight and unbroken, for which Joseph was grateful. In his mind, he could still hear the screams of the two criminals after their legs had been broken. Joseph had seen the mallet-wielding Roman pause in front of Jesus' cross, but when the soldier realized death had arrived ahead of him, he had passed on to the next man without breaking Jesus' legs.

"What shall we do about a burial chamber?" Nicodemus asked, suddenly aware of the critical issue.

"I have a new tomb nearby. It was made for myself, Nicodemus. We can place his body there."

"How near is it, Joseph?"

"Right over there. In the garden." (John 19:41; Luke 23:53; Matthew 27:60)

The two council members, together with the disciples of Jesus, supervised the placing of the corpse in the new tomb. The body was placed face up on a low stone niche that had been carved out of the limestone rock.

The burial party picked up the lighted torch and backed reverently out of the small antechamber. They reentered the outside garden area just as the sun touched the horizon. The great stone was rolled across the entrance.

Joseph and Nicodemus saw the women still watching. Mary Magdalene's face remained longest in their sight. Then, having done all they could, all of the friends and relatives of Jesus departed.

The garden tomb was deserted.

The sun had gone down. The Sabbath had begun. It was a long night.

The next day, the chief priests approached Pilate. "Sir," the spokesman began, "we remember that the deceiver, Jesus of Nazareth, said while he was yet alive, 'After three days I will rise again.' " (Matt. 27:63)

The governor was impatient. He had known nothing but trouble ever since the beginning of the affair.

"Governor, we would like you to command that the tomb be made secure until the third night."

"What for?"

"So that his disciples don't come by night and steal his body and then tell the people, 'He has risen from the dead.' " (Matt. 27:64)

Pilate waved an impatient hand at the chief priests and scribes. Anything he could do to head off more difficulties was in order. He snapped: "You have a watch! Go make it as secure as you can!" (Matt. 27:65)

A double precaution was taken. A squad of legionnaires was assigned to guard the tomb by watches. In addition to the troops, the religious leaders were allowed to secure the entrance to Jesus' tomb with a seal. This was a cylinder which was rolled into wet clay and allowed to harden. Roman officials often wore their personal seals on a cord around their necks. But Pilate's seal was probably a signet ring. It was pressed into wet clay to seal the entrance of the tomb where Jesus' body lay.

Before the day had ended, the hot sun had dried the clay. Anyone breaking the seal would be in serious trouble. However, there wasn't much likelihood of the seal being broken because of the patrolling soldiers in front of the tomb.

The day watch ended and the night watch began. Nothing transpired during the evening and midnight watches. Then the cock crowed and the bored and weary troops began to be impatient to be relieved of their posts.

It had been about thirty-six hours since Jesus of Nazareth had been entombed.

The guards were startled to feel another tremor of the earth, much like the one that had occurred on Friday afternoon at the crucifixion. But this tremor was followed by a snapping of the tomb's dried clay seals.

A moment later a brilliant burst of intense white light exploded from the tomb's interior.

The soldiers staggered backward, protecting their eyes from the flash. The great stone over the entrance of the burial vault rolled aside.

Inside the tomb, where it should have been pitch black, the burial shroud was plainly visible. It was faintly pulsating with a strange whiteness brighter than the linen itself.

However, there was no body inside it!

And there was something else: smoke, perhaps, or something burned ever so slightly.

The four Roman soldiers experienced all of this in a single, terrifying moment. Then the youngest man threw down his spear, dropped his curved shield, and ran screaming from the garden. His three companions followed.

In a few moments, silence had again settled over the burial site.

The faintly glowing burial cloth sagged in mute testimony that the body it had held was gone.

The tomb was empty.

12

ECHOES FROM
AN EMPTY TOMB

The Gospels record that Mary Magdalene came to the garden at dawn, or while it was still dark, on the day after the Sabbath. John mentions only Mary Magdalene as being at the tomb, but the synoptics name other women as well. Since John's narrative gives us a possible clue to the historical Jesus, we'll follow his version of what happened next.

Mary ran to Simon Peter and John and blurted out her discovery: "They have taken away the Lord out of the tomb! We don't know where they have laid him!" (John 20:2)

The two disciples ran together toward the garden. But John outran Peter and reached the sepulcher first. John stooped down and peered into the empty tomb. He saw the linen wrappings lying there, but did not enter. (John 20:4–5)

Then Peter arrived at the tomb and entered.

It was forbidden for Jews to handle burial cloths or other items considered "unclean." But Peter saw the linen wrappings and, lying by itself, the face-cloth that had been on his head. (John 20:5–7)

Then John entered the sepulcher. And when he

too had seen the burial cloths, he believed. (John 20: 6–8)

But Peter and John returned to their homes, leaving Mary Magdalene standing alone outside the tomb, weeping. Through her tears, she stooped to look again into the sepulcher. (John 20:10–11)

Two angels were sitting there. One sat at the head and the other at the feet of where Jesus' body had been.

One angel asked, "Woman, why are you weeping?" She replied, "Because they have taken away my Lord, and I don't know where they have laid him." (John 20:13)

As she said this, she turned around and saw Jesus standing there. But she didn't recognize him; she thought that he was the gardener.

Jesus asked, *"Woman, why are you weeping? Whom do you seek?"*

Mary answered, still unaware to whom she was talking, "Sir, if you have carried him away, tell me where you have laid him, and I will take him away." (John 20:15)

Jesus said, *"Mary!"*

Mary Magdalene turned and recognized Jesus. She cried out "Rabboni!" ("master" in Aramaic). (John 20:16)

He cautioned her, *"Don't touch me, for I haven't yet ascended to my Father! Go to my brethren and say to them, 'I ascend to my Father and your Father, and my God and your God.' "* (John 20:17)

Mary ran again to the disciples and told them that she had seen the Lord. She repeated Jesus' conversation with her, and what his message to them had been. (John 20:18)

According to Mark, the mourning and weeping disciples refused to believe that Jesus was alive and that Mary Magdalene had seen him. (Mark 16:10)

In the meantime, Jerusalem was abuzz with other excited conversations about the empty tomb and Jesus of Nazareth. Some of the guards who had fled from the garden before dawn reported to the chief priests what had happened. They then assembled with the elders and talked over the situation.

It was decided to give a large bribe to the soldiers.

"You are to say," the elders told the Roman guards, " 'his disciples came by night and stole him while we were asleep.' " (Matt. 28:13)

The soldiers took the money. It was better than being punished for deserting their posts.

The religious leaders cautioned the troop, "If any of this comes to the ears of Governor Pontius Pilate, we will win him over and keep you out of trouble." (Matt. 28:14)

The soldiers obeyed and spread the story that the chief priests had given them. This version of what had happened at the garden tomb was believed in from then on by those who deny Christ's resurrection.

Jesus' disciples spent that first day in mourning and in discussing the strange events—all except Judas Iscariot.

On Friday morning, after Jesus had been accused before Pilate, Judas was remorseful. He went to the chief priests and elders to return the thirty pieces of silver he had been paid for betraying his leader. "I have sinned by betraying innocent blood," Judas explained.

The religious leaders shrugged. "What is that to us?" (Matt. 27:3–4)

Judas threw the silver into the sanctuary and went out and hanged himself. (Matt. 27:5) Another version of the story has it that, having purchased a field with the silver, Judas fell "and all his bowels gushed out." (Acts 1:18)

Except for some post-resurrection New Testament accounts which we will cover in a later chapter, that is basically the story of Jesus of Nazareth as recorded in the Gospels. A clue to help us in our search for the historic Jesus is also included in the material we've covered so far in this chapter. We will also examine that later.

But let us first consider some new evidence in regard to the accuracy of the New Testament.

We have already established the fact that the historical context of the Bible is well authenticated by archaeological and other scientific evidence. But is there any specific archaeological, historical or other evidence of Jesus' existence?

Thallus, a secular chronicler who wrote in Greek about 52 AD, was believed to be a Samaritan.[1] Only fragments of his work remain. But in these there is a reference to the mysterious eclipse (if this is what it was) that occurred in April about 30 AD.

The commentaries of Josephus, the Jewish historian, on John the Baptist are authentic. Of his two references to Jesus, one is challenged while the second is undisputed.

In his *Antiquities of the Jews*, Josephus has written:

> Now there was about this time a certain Jesus, a wise man, if it be lawful to call him a man, for he was a doer of wonderful works, a teacher of such men as receive the truth with pleasure.
>
> He drew over to him both many of the Jews, and many of the Gentiles.
>
> He was the Christ, and when Pilate, at the suggestion of the principal men among us, had condemned him to the cross, those that loved him at the first did not forsake him; for he appeared to them alive again the third day; as the divine prophets had foretold these and ten thousand other wonderful things concerning him. And the tribe of Christians so named from him are not extinct to this day.[2]

The authenticity of this passage has been challenged as a later interpolation by someone other than Josephus. Why, it has been asked, would Josephus, a Jew, have given only a brief coverage to the life of one whom he supposedly called "the Christ"?

Josephus wrote extensively about persons who played a comparatively minor role in history; men who were shepherds, for example, and set crowns on their own heads and declared themselves kings. Common sense suggests that those who claim this passage is spurious have a certain amount of logic on their side.

But what about the second reference to Jesus in the *Antiquities?* This entry was made after Festus died (his name occurs later in the New Testament) and Caesar sent Albinus to Judea as procurator.

This second passage in which Josephus refers to Jesus indicates that Annas "was a bold man in his temper, and very insolent," a Sadducee and one of the five sons of Annas, the high priest before whom Jesus had first been haled. While Albinus was traveling toward Jerusalem to succeed Festus, Annas the younger seized the high priesthood and "assembled the Sanhedrin of the judges and brought before them the brother of Jesus, who was called Christ, whose name was James, and some others, and when he had formed an accusation against them as breakers of the law, he delivered them to be stoned."[3]

Origen, an early church father who wrote about 230 AD, commented on Josephus' references to Jesus in *Antiquities of the Jews*. He argues that the Jewish historian reflects what was then a commonly-held belief as to the cause of the destruction of the temple and Jerusalem under Titus in 70 AD. Origen wrote: "These miseries befell the Jews by way of revenge for James the Just, who was the brother of Jesus that was called Christ; because they had slain him who was a most righteous person."[4]

According to Protestants, James was Jesus' brother, while according to Catholics, they were cousins.

The great apostle, Paul, who carried the Christian message to the Gentile world while the apostles who carried it to the Jewish world remained in Jerusalem, mentions James as well: "Then three years later I went up to Jerusalem to become acquainted with Cephas [Peter], and stayed with him about fifteen days. But I did not see any other of the apostles except James, the Lord's brother." (Gal. 1:18–19)

The Gospels repeatedly place James first in the

list of Jesus' siblings, as would naturally be done if James were the oldest. It is obvious that Jesus' brothers and sisters did not believe that he was the Messiah early in his ministry. Perhaps even his mother doubted Jesus once. (Mark 3:21, 31)

Eusebius, a later church historian, indicates that by tradition James was bishop of Jerusalem. Certainly the Scriptures show that James was a leader of the church in Jerusalem until the destruction of the city and temple. James is said to have died about 62 AD.

Hegesippus extends Joesphus' account of James' death. The later report undoubtedly depended upon tradition or material not now available. James, like most of the early believers who were soon called Christians, was a Jew. But the Jewish authorities caused James to stand upon a temple wing where the angry people threw him down and stoned him because of his testimony about Jesus.

Other non-biblical chroniclers have left records which do not necessarily prove Jesus of Nazareth actually lived, but are empirical proofs that many people of that immediate time were positive he had. They were so sure Jesus was what he had claimed to be that these people died for their faith.

Julius Africanus (*circa* 221 AD) cites Thallus, who wrote around 52 AD, as the first non-Jew to mention Christ: "Thallus, in the third book of his histories, explains away this darkness as an eclipse of the sun—unreasonably, as it seems to me."

Thallus' original works are mostly lost, but the portions that remain suggest that he challenged that a solar eclipse could have occurred at the time of a full moon. However, while this is a logical explanation for the eclipse at Jesus' death, the New Testament does not clearly say whether it was an eclipse or something else.

Josephus was commander of the Jewish forces in Galilee during the war against the Romans in 66 AD, so he was on the scene when the final conflict began. His references to Jesus have already been noted. But it is interesting that the Arabic text of the same challenged quote about Jesus being the Christ is softened to read: "He was perhaps the Messiah concerning whom the prophets had recounted wonders."[5]

Cornelius Tacitus (*circa* 112 AD) wrote of Nero's reign and of how Christians were blamed for the terrible fire in Rome in 64 AD. To shift the blame from himself, the mad emperor falsely charged with the guilt, and punished with the most exquisite tortures, the persons commonly called Christians, who were hated for their enormities. Christus, the founder of the name, was put to death by Pontius Pilate, procurator of Judea in the reign of Tiberius; but the pernicious superstition, repressed for a time, broke out again, not only through Judea, where the mischief originated, but through the city of Rome itself.[6]

Suetonius (*circa* 120 AD), a Roman historian during the reign of Emperor Hadrian, has two references to Christ (whom he calls "Chrestus," an alternative spelling of "Christus," still used today):

> As the Jews were making constant disturbances at the instigation of Chrestus, he [Emperor Claudius] expelled them from Rome.[7]
> Punishment by Nero was inflicted on the Christians, a class of men given to a new and mischievous superstition.[8]

Pliny the Younger wrote a lengthy letter about 112 AD when he was governor of Bithynia in Asia Minor. He sought the opinion of Emperor Trajan in dealing with the Christians. Until he wrote this letter, Pliny had been persecuting and killing the Christians. The number of martyrs was so great that Pliny wondered if he should only kill certain Christians, rather than all who professed a belief in Christ.

The Christians, Pliny noted "were in the habit of meeting on a certain fixed day before it was light, when they sang in alternate verse a hymn to Christ as a god, and bound themselves, by a solemn oath, not to do any wicked deeds, but never to commit any fraud, theft, adultery, never to falsify their word, not to deny a trust when they should be called upon to deliver it."[9]

Justin Martyr, writing about 150 AD to Emperor Antoninus Pius, referred to a report by Pontius Pilate which presumably was in the imperial archives. Mentioning the nailing of Jesus' hands and feet and the gambling for his clothes, as recorded in the Scriptures, Justin Martyr added: ". . . that these things were so, you may learn from the 'Acts' which were recorded under Pontius Pilate."[10]

Tertullian (*circa* 197 AD) mentions a reputed exchange between Pontius Pilate and Tiberius Caesar:

> Tiberius accordingly, in those days the Christian name having made its entry into the world, having himself received intelligence of the truth of Christ's divinity, brought the matter before the Senate, with his own decision in favor of Christ. The Senate, because it had not given the approval itself, rejected this proposal. Caesar held to his opinion, threatening wrath against all the accusers of the Christians.[11]

There is no point in going beyond the second century for passages that prove that near-contemporaries accepted without question that there had been a Jesus of Nazareth and that his followers were spreading rapidly, in spite of being persecuted for their beliefs. Indeed, the Hebrew *Talmud* provides conclusive proof that Jesus of Nazareth really existed as an historical person:

> On the eve of Passover they hanged Yeshu [of Nazareth] and the herald went before him for forty days saying [Yeshu of Nazareth] is going forth to be stoned in that he hath practiced sorcery and beguiled and led astray Israel. Let everyone knowing aught in his defense come and plead for him. But they found naught in his defense and hanged him on the eve of Passover.[12]

Nothing can be taken for granted in researching as sensitive a subject as the Jesus of history. But while some of our investigations disclosed myths where facts had been assumed, a great deal of confirming data outside the New Testament was also turned up.

For example, the many visitors to the State of Israel today can see the town in Galilee where Jesus is supposed to have grown up. The Sea of Galilee, where Jesus is said to have walked on the water, the Mount of Olives, and the Garden of Gethsemane are popular sites.

The Gabbatha, or pavement where Jesus suffered under Pilate, has recently been unearthed.

But where is Calvary, or Golgotha? There is a place called Gordon's Calvary, which few serious scholars consider as likely. The true site is subject to speculation, but many believe it is under the Ecce Homo Convent in Jerusalem.

Everyone visiting the famous city today wants to see the Wailing Wall. This recalls a prophecy made by Jesus to his disciples that the time was coming when not one stone of the temple would be left standing.

That came true in 70 AD when the Roman general, Titus, unintentionally allowed his troops to destroy the magnificent thirty-five-acre temple which King Herod had started building. The polished marble stones, the gold and precious stones, had all been destroyed by the rampaging legionnaires.

The Western Wall, which still remains, was not a part of the temple, but was actually a part of the wall from Herod's palace. Every last stone of the temple was cast down, exactly as Jesus had predicted.

To many people, what happens in Jerusalem in the coming years will be of vital importance because of many prophecies some people believe have not yet been fulfilled. These have to do with a world battle of nations near Jerusalem.

If these predictions are true, what happens in Israel will some day affect everyone reading this book, and millions of others around the world who may never have heard of it, or Jesus of Nazareth.

If some things Jesus said have come true, why shouldn't the others eventually also prove true?

It is a sobering thought, especially when it is recalled that the Jews lost their temple and city in 70 AD and were finally ejected from Jerusalem in 134 AD, not to return for nearly 2,000 years. They returned as a nation in 1948, something unknown in the history of mankind, and retook all of Jerusalem in 1967.

But the clock of Jerusalem and Israel continues to beat time—according to biblical scholars.

And so our search for the historical Jesus takes on new meaning, and brings us to the one possible piece of physical evidence which still exists today. Its story is so dramatic that some of the world's best scientists are now checking its authenticity.

We refer to the so-called burial shroud of Christ.

13

A SECRET IN
AN ITALIAN ATTIC

If a single piece of physical evidence of Jesus' resurrection exists, how did it survive nearly 2,000 years?

If there is such a relic from the most sensational single incident in all of history (assuming that Jesus really did rise from the dead), where did it come from in the first place?

Why doesn't the whole world know about such a remarkable object?

And most important of all, how can it be proven whether this possible piece of physical evidence is genuine or a very clever hoax?

We asked ourselves some of these questions as our search for the historical Jesus took us into an examination of the highly controversial Shroud of Turin. This is a Roman Catholic relic which some claim is the burial shroud of Jesus.

Some highly respected scientists believe the relic is genuine. Investigations of the shroud have been conducted with instruments as technologically advanced as those which landed a man on the moon and gave us photo enhancements from "fly-bys" of such distant planets as Mars and Saturn. So we checked into the possibility that this artifact is the last piece of physical evidence about the historic Jesus.

Our story begins in a most unlikely place: an attic in Italy.

There was absolutely no reason to suspect that lawyer-photographer Seconda Pia was about to make a sensational discovery that day in May 1898. His findings would touch off a controversy which would rock the Catholic Church and even reverberate throughout the scientific world. The controversy is more widespread now, and it continues to grow after more than three-quarters of a century. People everywhere are even more fascinated by the unexplained mystery which literally developed under a red kerosene lamp in an Italian darkroom.

It was uncomfortable in the converted closet which the tall, slender native of Piedmont had made in the attic of his home in Turin. Pia, barely visible in the lamp's red glow, leaned anxiously over the oxolate of iron solution. He ignored the sharp fumes that irritated his eyes and nose.

Beside him a short, wiry teenaged boy impatiently brushed the same fumes from his dark eyes.

"Careful of the lamp, Tony!" Seconda warned.

The youth moved a half step away from the small, red-shaded lamp sitting on a shelf at eye level. "See anything yet, Signor Pia?"

Pia shook his head. "Not yet. Just see the silver particles sloughing off the glass negative. But soon, I think, we will see something."

Both continued to watch intently the silver particles vanishing from the large glass plate into the developing solution.

"It is taking such a long time, Signor Pia," the teenaged assistant complained. "Are you sure everything was done right?"

The tall man smiled. "I hope so, Tony."

"Photography is such a new science. Perhaps there was a mistake. After all, there were so many problems . . ."

"I know the problems, my young friend. Rest assured, I have been most careful. Now, unless you can remember something we did wrong, let's save our breath. This attic closet is not the world's best place for holding a pleasant conversation."

The teenager nodded. "That's true, Signor Pia. I will be glad when we have finished and can see what the camera has caught. Just think! The world's first photograph of the most sacred relic in the Church!"

"You're still talking, Tony," the tall man said in gently reproving tones, gently agitating the glass plate.

The excited youth closed his mouth and leaned closer to the developing tray. "Signor, I see something!"

"You are right, Tony! The camera has caught something! But . . . ?"

"But what, Signor Pia?"

"Something is wrong, Tony! See?"

"I see something forming on the negative, Signor . . . but I see nothing wrong!"

"Ah, but you do, Tony! You have already said it! You see something forming on the negative. And what does it look like?"

The youth frowned in the red lamp's faint glow. Then he straightened triumphantly to face up to his taller companion. "This one is not like the others we have developed! This one does not look like a negative—it looks like a positive!"

"That's it, Tony! We are getting a positive image where we should be getting a negative! And that's impossible!"

The youth and the man turned in silent wonder to watch the large plate-glass negative. Slowly, before their eyes, dark spots formed until the faint image of a man shimmered through the oxolate of iron solution.

"Mama mia!" The youth looked sharply up at the older man. "That is not what we saw when we took the photograph a while ago!"

"No, Tony," the lawyer-photographer mused softly. "That is not what we saw—but it is what the camera saw!"

By now, the image was quite clear. Where a negative with reversed streaks of light that later would appear dark in a negative print should have appeared, there was exposed a positive print of a man lying prone.

He wore shoulder-length hair, a beard, and a mustache. The face was serene, with the eyes apparently closed in death. The body was nude. The hands were crossed over the groin. The right foot was slightly raised.

In an instant, the two Italians saw what appeared to be distinguishing blood marks on the image forming in the developing solution. There were marks around the scalp such as a crown of thorns would have made. There was a large open wound on the chest near the heart. A nailhole could be seen in the wrist and feet. There were crisscrossed marks over the body that appeared to be bloody lacerations where the flesh had been ripped and torn by a cruel whip.

"Mama mia!" the younger man exclaimed. "What have we done?"

"Ah," the taller man said reverently. "We have taken the first photograph of our Lord!"

The startling news raced through Turin where the so-called Shroud of Turin had been housed for three centuries. Some cried, "Miracle!" while others yelled, "Fraud!" The controversy remained inside the Roman Catholic Church for some time, but eventually spread outside. The authenticity of the Shroud of Turin soon involved the prestigious French Academy of Sciences.

Then the controversy spread farther and wider until the world's finest minds and the latest scientific studies were focused on the questions raised by Seconda Pia's photographs:

Was this really the winding sheet in which Jesus Christ had been buried before he rose on the third day?

Was the shroud a clever hoax; and if so, who had perpetrated it and why?

What is the evidence that Jesus Christ actually existed as an historic person?

Was the shroud a piece of physical evidence of Jesus' life?

Was the shroud a picture of Christ's last week on earth?

The search for the historical Jesus could logically be said to have begun with the 1898 photographic study of the Shroud of Turin. That was the spark that ignited a global controversy which is still ardently pursued today.

The hapless lawyer-photographer was haled before important assemblies to clarify the situation. A chairman looked at his panel of experts and then spoke to the man who had begun it all.

"Signor Pia, let us start with possible errors in your darkroom," the chairman said. "After all, photography is a new field, and perhaps there was a mistake made there."

Seconda Pia stood as he had already done before church officials and began again to explain.

"Less than three-quarters of a century before—in 1826—the Frenchman, Joseph Nicéphore Niepce, took the first known photograph. He continued to pioneer photography until his death in 1833.

"Niepce was a partner with Louis Jacques Mandé Daguerre. Daguerre went on to be recognized as the inventor of the first process of photography. Naturally, the first photographs—or daguerreotypes—were mostly of people instead of buildings, since only one copy could be made."

The chairman interrupted: "Yes! Yes! We quite understand! But we are more interested in how you proceeded in taking the first pictures of this—this so-called image of Christ. As you know, Signor Pia, those who have seen the shroud with their own eyes have not seen such images as your camera has recorded here."

The tall Italian sighed and recalled again how the whole situation had developed. "Perhaps we should begin with the shroud itself. I'm sure you gentlemen are familiar with the fact that this is the most sacred relic in all Christendom."

The interrogators glanced at each other and nodded. Pia continued. "Let me begin at the day of the Crucifixion. The Scriptures record how Joseph of Arimathea and Nicodemus had claimed our Lord's body from Pilate following Jesus' death on the cross. Do you all remember?"

The men somberly nodded in unison. Jesus' body was hastily wrapped in a new linen winding sheet which Joseph of Arimathea had purchased. Since it was so close to the Sabbath and the Passover of the Jews, the crucified body was not prepared for burial in the usual Jewish manner. Instead it was laid in a new tomb with the intention of completing the traditional anointing after the Sabbath. Pia said, "You gentlemen know what happened the third day."

The researchers again nodded. The resurrection story was familiar to every one of them. About sunrise, women carrying ointments had gone early to the rock sepulcher. They had found the stone rolled away, and an angel had announced: "He is not here! He is risen!"

The French Academy of Sciences boasted a lot of freethinkers who didn't necessarily believe that Jesus of Nazareth had really risen. Among those learned men was Yves Delage, an avowed agnostic. His laboratory was chosen for critical examination of the shroud, based entirely on Pia's photographs. He was joined at the Sorbonne by Paul Vignon and other equally worldly and distinguished academicians.

But after eighteen months of study, both men were believers. Vignon went on to spend years studying the shroud and writing about it. Delage startled the world with his testimony on the afternoon of April 21, 1902.[1]

The 80 best scientific and academic brains in all France sat at green-covered tables. About 200 spectators were squashed together along benches by the walls, below the high-ceilinged, narrow chamber.

Bearded, dark-suited Delage adjusted his small wire-rimmed glasses and began to testify of the findings made by him and other highly qualified members of the prestigious academy.

After his introductory remarks, the scientist declared: "The question poses itself as to how the image was made."[2] He didn't really know, but the really important question had been resolved in his mind.

Using fellow-researcher Vignon's materials, Delage led up to a flat statement: "The conviction results that the image of the shroud is not a painting."[3]

The rising excitement of the crowd was evident as the known agnostic and freethinker began to summarize his findings. His conclusion rocked the room and the scientific community: "The man of the shroud was the Christ!"[4]

Although this was primarily a Catholic-oriented story, *The New York Times* carried a piece on the significance of the report by Paul Vignon and Yves Delage. *Scientific American* also reported on the relic.

The critics, however, jumped to the attack almost at once. Some of the most famous of these detractors of the shroud's authenticity came from within the church. And they based their conclusions, they said, on the solid foundation of historical research.

The most qualified of these early detractors was Cyr Ulysse Chevalier, a French Catholic priest.[5] He triumphantly presented quotes from the past—some 550 years—which claimed the shroud was a fraud.

But what was the basis for this charge of deceit? What was the relic's history before 1355? Where had it been—if it was really the genuine cloth in which Jesus had been buried—for nearly 1,400 years?

Researchers started digging.

The results have been amazing. A great deal has been learned about the crucifixion.

These sincere efforts to prove—one way or another—if the relic is genuine helped turn up a number of curiously related legends and stories. Some of them are still repeated today in standard reference works. There are variations on the story, but the essential elements remain.

*   *   *

Abgar V ruled at Edessa (now Urfa, Turkey), an independent Mesopotamian kingdom, at the time Jesus of Nazareth was alive. Eusebius of Caesarea in the early fourth century listed an exchange of letters supposedly sent between Jesus and the king of Osrhoene.[6]

The king asked Jesus to come cure him of an illness. The healer from Nazareth did not come, but indicated he would send a disciple, Thaddaeus (Addai), after his ascension.

There were still no church buildings, for the gathered body of believers *was* the church for about 200 years. But many converts were made when Thaddaeus (one of Jesus' lesser-known disciples, who is also believed to have been called Lebbaeus and, possibly, Judas the son of James) arrived in Edessa. He was accompanied by a male Greek companion. By then, Abgar was close to death. He received the apostle with a wan smile which vanished when he learned Jesus had been crucified.

"Ah, my friend Thaddaeus! How great is the sadness you bring me with this news!"

The disciple who had traveled so far shook his head. "You do not understand, O great king of Edessa! This same Jesus who was crucified, dead and buried, has risen to life again!"

The Mesopotamian king managed to raise his head from his pillow. "How is that possible?"

Quickly, Thaddaeus recounted the trial, death, burial, and resurrection of the man from Nazareth.

"Then this Jesus is alive, even though he was dead?" the king asked weakly.

"Yes, O King Abgar. And because he lives, those who believe in him shall also live with him some day."

The king sighed. "I would like to know more about this Jesus who was dead and now lives, but my time is short. The court physicians tell me I am upon my death-bed. But where I go, I shall not live again."

The apostle hesitated, then asked: "King Abgar, do you believe in this Jesus whom I told you about?"

The king managed to gather his strength. "I believed enough that I have sent letters to him, as you know. But how can I send another letter to him where he has gone—to sit on the right hand of God, as you explained?"

"You cannot send to him, but he has sent to you. My Gentile companion here has brought you something."

Thaddaeus' Greek friend stepped forward and presented a cloth to the stricken monarch. The Gentile bowed and returned to his position.

"Ah!" Abgar exclaimed. "What have we here? A cloth with an image of a man . . ."

The king's voice trailed off. He weakly lifted the gift to his cheeks and collapsed upon the pillow.

But Abgar was not dead. According to legend, as he touched the cloth to his face, he miraculously revived and was soon totally recovered.

There is some credence to this possibility reported in the New Testament. Paul the Apostle, who had been Saul the strict Pharisee before his conversion to Christianity, had a scriptural record of miracles at Ephesus. The Book of Acts reports: "And God was performing extraordinary miracles by the hands of Paul, so that handkerchiefs or aprons were even carried from his body to the sick, and the diseases left them and the evil spirits went out." (Acts 19:11–12)

According to Edessan legend, a church was begun as a result of the cloth which the apostle carried to the king, effecting a cure of his diseases.

But was this cloth the same one which the Catholic Church today considers the most sacred relic?

There is no way of knowing, but lots of research by qualified scholars and writers has turned up some fascinating possibilities that the legendary cloth was a link to today's Shroud of Turin.

Not long after Abgar's miraculous recovery, the Romans invaded his small, independent kingdom. The king ordered the cloth—then called the Image of Edessa—to be hidden so it would not fall into the hands of the invaders.

The possibility is advanced that the cloth was

placed in a large, oblong box, hastily buried in the city's walls, and bricked over. There, it seems, the cloth remained until 525 AD when a devastating flood swept through Edessa. As engineers worked with stonemasons to repair the wall after the flood, a workman came upon the box. It was opened and the workers looked down into a cloth which somehow retained the faintest image of a man—but not just any man, judging from the wounds.

This cloth was called *acheiropoitos,* a Greek word meaning "not made with hands." It was acclaimed as "the true likeness of Christ" and hailed as Christendom's greatest relic.[7]

But now something unique was noted on the cloth. It bore the facial, but not the bodily, likeness of the crucified Jesus.

The Mandylion, a Greek word for a cloth or veil, is also defined as a kind of loose coat or cassock. It was later sleeveless and became a kind of overcoat for menservants and soldiers. As defined by one nineteenth-century reference book, it is "a large garment full of folds."[8]

Full of folds.

Could it be that the Image of Edessa had become the Mandylion through folding the larger cloth (as might have been done when it was hastily hidden in the wall) in such a manner that only the face was visible when it was rediscovered nearly 500 years later?

Admittedly, this is speculative, but as later scientific testimony about the Shroud of Turin will show, there is something very special about the history of the relic. Modern technology can tell us where the shroud had been before its known history started 500 years ago.

But if the Image of Edessa and the Mandylion are the same, how did they get to be the Shroud of Turin?

And how can anything as speculative as legends and apocryphal material tell us anything to help us in our search for the historic Jesus?

It is somewhat like reconstructing pieces of a mystery puzzle. The mute testimony of the Shroud of Turin may tell us more about Jesus of Nazareth than perhaps any resource outside the Bible.

So let us follow the centuries-old clues to their startling conclusion.

14

THE HISTORY
AND MYSTERY
OF THE SHROUD

To millions of Protestant Americans, the idea of a religious relic is repugnant. The Catholic Church, in recent years, has down-played objects of veneration. Such negative views of relics such as the Shroud of Turin apparently had their roots in the old Mosaic laws forbidding image worship. The Catholics naturally do not consider that this is what they do; Protestants take no chances and entirely avoid anything resembling such a suggestion. Yet the controversy is not new.

And it is this controversy that provides a clue that may help us in our search for the historic Jesus.

As the Eastern and Western branches of Catholicism moved toward the rupture which was eventually to split them forever—long before the Protestant Reformation—a controversy arose over icons and relics.

In essence, the Image of Edessa and the Mandylion were relics. A relic is an object which is considered to be sacred in itself. A great historical clash occurred between the Roman Catholics and Eastern Catholics in the eighth and ninth centuries over such relics.

The best known, perhaps, of early relics was the one called "Veronica's Veil." The name grew out of *vera icon,* meaning "true image." Veronica's veil was not merely an icon—i.e. an image of a sacred object; it was considered to be an object with supernatural power of its own. This is evidenced by the way the Image of Edessa was used in war.

Shortly after the Mandylion was rediscovered in the walls of Edessa, the town in present-day Turkey was attacked by the Persians. As the siege stretched on, the defenders paraded the image about the city. The Persians were repulsed. The Mandylion got the credit.

The Byzantine Empire had lost Edessa by the time the iconoclastic fury (iconoclasm is disbelief in all images) had spent itself between 725 and 845 AD. But in 943, Emperor Romanus Lecapenus of Constantinople ordered his troops to invade Syria and recover the cloth. The iconoclasts of Orthodox Constantinople were offered a couple of frauds, but the army refused to depart until the true Mandylion was surrendered. The cloth apparently remained in Constantinople for the next several centuries, where it was paraded around the city walls as a supernatural defense against various attackers.

And it stayed there until 1204 when the Fourth Crusaders were diverted from their original mission to free the Holy Land from the Moslems. The Western Christians, with their red-cross symbols painted on breastplates, turned on the Eastern Christians in a savage display which was to have many repetitions in succeeding centuries: believers fighting believers who didn't believe exactly the same things.

Constantinople had become a haven for many of the most valuable Christian relics in the centuries since the Crusades had begun. The Holy Land had fallen to the "infidels." The Crusades were launched, at least ostensibly, to regain the sacred birthplace of Christendom, but they were mainly unsuccessful.

In those years, roughly from the sixth century on, depictions of Jesus had changed dramatically. The Scriptures gave absolutely no physical description of

Jesus. So artists began to represent him according to their imaginations.

Historically, the early sketches showed him as a youth, clean-shaven, which no Jew of his time was likely to be. But this innocent, beardless young man of religious art vanished after about the sixth century. In his stead, artists began drawing a man with strikingly similar features.

And researchers today have noted that those similarities appeared to be based on the present Shroud of Turin.

But unless those artists had something like the Image of Edessa or Mandylion, folded and not full-length as the Shroud is, how did these startling similarities originate?

Some books today like Robert K. Wilcox's *Shroud*[1] have detailed those same features which began appearing after the sixth century—about the time the Mandylion was known to have reappeared after vanishing centuries before.

Paul Vignon, a French scientist at the time Seconda Pia's first photographs were made in 1898, spent a lot of time comparing icons in Paris depositories.[2] He found, for example, that about 80 percent of the Byzantine icons had the same V-shaped mark at the nose between the eyes.

The other similarities Vignon noted were a lack of ears and neck, a "forked" beard, a "truncated" mustache, a straight nose, one raised eyebrow, and enlarged nostrils. There were also what seemed to be swollen cheeks and a bruised forehead.[3]

Tracing the icons back through the centuries to their apparent origin, the French investigator saw that the oldest icons were apparently copied from the Image of Edessa!

This doesn't prove conclusively that the Image or Mandylion was the source of the centuries of artists' renderings, but it is enough of a coincidence to cause serious researchers to ponder the matter.

*   *   *

Following these indistinct clues back through the centuries in our search for the historic Jesus takes us to the Fourth Crusade when Western Christians turned their military might on Eastern Christians at the sack of Constantinople. Chroniclers of the period record something which suggests what happened to the Mandylion before the Shroud of Turin made its appearance in recorded history.

Only one immediate reference was made to a possible burial cloth in Constantinople before the siege. In 1201, the patriarch of that city and head of the Eastern church, Nicolas Mesarites, catalogued the relics there. There was more than one, judging from his comment: "They are of linen, of cheap material, such as was available. They still smell of perfume. They have defied decay because they enveloped the ineffable, naked, myrrh-covered corpse after the Passion."[4]

The patriarch made no mention of images. But he used the word "naked," which accords with the image on the Shroud of Turin. Traditionally, Jesus has never been depicted as naked. So it is a curious coincidence.

Robert de Clari, a member of the Fourth Crusade, left a record of his participation in the 1204 sack of the richest city in Christendom. His report is augmented by the Comte de Villehardouin.[5]

The Venetians and the French Crusaders had been blessed by the pope as they headed for Alexandria with the intention of capturing Egypt and splitting the Moslem world in half.[6] They had taken up the cross, and sworn on it and the Holy Gospels to bypass Christian territory without shedding blood. The Crusaders had sworn to take up arms only against the Saracens. The Crusaders were to keep themselves chaste while they bore the cross and to defend Jesus' tomb.[7]

But the possibility of gain and a religious difference turned the expedition aside. It sailed for Constantinople, the capital of the Byzantine Empire which had successfully resisted sixteen previous sieges over 900 years. Part of this successful resistance to attack was attributed by the Greek defenders to the many holy relics which were periodically displayed to help defend the city.

The Latin attackers reasoned that the Greek Orthodox Church had broken from the true Western Church at Rome and deserved to be punished. But the victorious attackers might carry off the city's plunder, too.

On the morning of June 22, 1203, the great armada of 450 warships and other vessels moved under sail and oar to the wide Dardanelles toward the walled city. The craft took the Sea of Marmora right up to the many gates, especially aiming for the Golden Gate at the tip of the peninsula, called the Horn.[8]

The galleys with their rowers, the *huissiers* or *palanders* with their landing-craft duties of carrying horses and men, plus the transports and merchant ships, sailed right up to the towers and began the assault. They splashed across the muddy flatlands toward the walls. Sappers under hard hide shelters began digging under the walls. Siege guns were tugged right up to the walls where rocks thrown from above began smashing them.

The famous Greek fire rained down on the ships which had some protection from the hides they had erected in the rigging, but not enough. The first day's assault was beaten back.

The Latin priests had some morale building to do that night. The Crusaders had violated their oath and their fellow believers had repulsed them. But the clerics, looking over the French knights and their horses, the foot soldiers with their red crosses on their breasts, and the sailors in their dirty uniforms, exhorted them as to the rightness of their cause: "The people of Constantinople were no more than heretics, for they did not accept the rule of Rome. For this reason it was the soldiers' duty to give battle. Far from being a sin, it was on the contrary a pious act."

After a couple of days of preparation and repairing damage, the Venetians and Frenchmen attacked again.

This time, the Crusaders used tubes in the ships'

assault ramps to send Greek fire back at the defenders. However, as Robert de Clari noted, "the fire had no effect on the wooden towers for they were all sheathed in skins."

The noisy battle continued with stone-throwing catapults from the defenders blending their noise with the pealing of warning church bells, blaring trumpets, and everywhere the cries of men dying in war. But this time the elements aided the attackers.

A northerly wind combined with a series of sea-breakers from the half-mile of open sea, forcing two lashed-together siege ships so close to the walls that their landing ramp and one defense tower were equal. Grappling irons were tossed from the ship and the tower became a strong holding unit. The Crusaders poured off the ships and across the tower. The defenders were slowly beaten back. Another tower was similarly attacked.

Meanwhile, foot soldiers ignored burning pitch dumped from the walls to smash in a city gate with pickaxes and battering rams. They poured through the breach, followed by knights, and joined up with the armored troops who had clambered from the ships to the towers.

Not even the Eastern Christian nuns were safe from the Western men with the cross of Christ on their chests. Horses were ridden into churches to help carry off the plunder. Nicetas Choniates, the Greek historian,[9] said of the French and Venetian victors: "They respected nothing! Neither the churches, nor the sacred images of Christ and His saints. They acted like enemies of the cross. They committed atrocities upon men, respectable women, virgins and young girls."

While nuns were being raped, convents and monasteries pillaged, and the famous altar of the Cathedral of Santa Sophia broken up,[10] Robert de Clari, the French Crusader, came upon a treasury of religious artifacts. He found 30 chapels in the palace of Boucoleon, 500 rooms richly decorated, plus the holy chapel with silver nails and hinges.

I cannot begin to tell you how beautiful and grand this whole building was! We found many rich relics there, among them two pieces of the True Cross, as thick as a man's leg and about three feet long. Then there was the iron head of the lance which pierced Our Lord's side, and the nails which were stuck through His hands and feet, a phial containing some of His blood, and the tunic that He wore.[11]

The likelihood of anything among these articles being genuine is remote. Some of these relics today repose in famous European Catholic churches.

Venice became famous for its craftsmen who imitated the great and priceless treasures stolen from Constantinople. The works of Byzantine artisans were copied and distributed throughout the cities of the West.

But one remark by de Clari provides a possible clue in our search for the historic Jesus. He wrote about a church which they called My Lady Saint Mary of Blachernae, where was kept the *sydoine* in which Our Lord had been wrapped, which stood up straight every Friday so that the features of Our Lord could be plainly seen there. And no one, either Greek or French, ever knew what became of the *sydoine* after the city was taken.[12]

That is the last known reference to the relic until a controversy in the mid 1300's suggested that the shroud may have again come to light. It is speculated that an unknown knight from Constantinople carried the artifact back to France where it stirred up a controversy which exists to this day.

But that controversy gives us another link in our search for the historic Jesus.

In 1389, the bishop of Troyes, Pierre d'Arcis, was angry because crowds were flocking to the town of Lirey to see a relic claimed to be the burial shroud of Christ.[13] D'Arcis' wrath was aroused because his permission had not been obtained for the exhibit. Instead, Geoffrey de Charny had gone over the bishop's head to Pierre de Thury, a cardinal and legate of the pope to King Charles VI of France.

Pope Clement VII had given permission to exhibit "a semblance or representation of the *sudarium* of our Lord."[14] The king's permission had also been given in writing.

The bishop of Troyes' letter to Pope Clement VII was intended to stop the Lirey exhibition. To do that, he needed proof that the shroud was a fraud.

The d'Arcis letter referred to Henri de Poitiers, who had been bishop of Troyes about 34 years earlier, in 1355. He had granted permission for the first exhibition of the relic to Geoffrey de Charny in Lirey. De Charny was killed in 1356, but not before he came into possession of what may be the most unique artifact in the Catholic church.[15]

How did he get the shroud? He never said. He was a French knight who had once been a prisoner of war in Britain. The king of France had ransomed him for gold, so de Charny seems to have been of some importance.

Records from 1343 to 1356 disclose that de Charny had endowed a Lirey church. There is no hint that the shroud was involved, although some researchers have suggested that the knight had the church erected especially for the relic.

Philip VI had allowed income to be diverted to help the church. Popes Clement VI and Innocent VI had approved the situation. Henri de Poitiers had also approved.

But some 34 years later, d'Arcis attempted to stop the exhibition of the shroud at Lirey by accusing de Poitiers of forgery: "Eventually, after diligent inquiry and examination, he discovered the fraud and how the said cloth had been cunningly painted, the truth being attested by the artist who had painted it; to wit, that it was a work of human skill and not miraculously wrought or bestowed."[16]

Bishop d'Arcis added that the investigation had

caused the cloth to be withdrawn from view and "kept hidden afterwards for 34 years or thereabouts down to the present year."[17] Now it was being exhibited again, and without the bishop's permission. He wanted the display stopped at once. Instead, it continued on exhibition until the bishop, now even more angry, asked the king to intervene on his behalf.

A still further blow came when Clement VII (one of two contenders for the papacy, and known to history as the "Anti-Pope") ordered d'Arcis to "perpetual silence."[18]

But he wouldn't remain quiet as long as the Lirey exhibition continued. The ringing controversy has left open possibilities for our search.

Questions arise. Did Henri de Poitiers really conduct an investigation? If so, who confessed to being the artist who made the forgery? Why did d'Arcis not offer names and other specifics?

In light of later scientific evidence that it is impossible for the image on the Shroud of Turin to be a painting, the angry bishop of Troyes would have done well to document his claims.

It was this letter which sparked the controversy after the startling disclosure by the agnostic, Yves Delage, that "the man in the shroud was the Christ." The man leading the counterattack was Canon Ulysse Chevalier.

The 57-year-old French priest was professor of ecclesiastical history at the Catholic University of Lyon when he launched his first attack against the shroud's authenticity.

By 1899, a year after Pia's first photographs had been taken, Chevalier had written an article which drew on the 1877 article by another prelate, Charles Lalore. He offered no proof except Bishop d'Arcis' angry letter of 488 years before. Chevalier's principal evidence was also this same letter.

Chevalier, an acknowledged authority on Roman Catholic church history, repeatedly wrote articles condemning the shroud's authenticity, but he offered no new evidence. He repeated Lalore's claims, which were themselves based on d'Arcis' letter, and which offered no empirical proof.

Other Catholic priests, notably the Englishman, Herbert Thurston, added their protests to the Frenchman, Chevalier. The net result was that a number of people who wouldn't have otherwise cared began to dig into the shroud's history.

That history was very uncertain until 1578 when the shroud was brought to the Chapel of St. John the Baptist in Turin, where Seconda Pia had photographed it in 1898. There were only questions and partial answers before that.

Were the Image of Edessa and the Mandylion the same?

Was it really the same shroud as the one seen by Robert de Clari in 1204 when the Crusaders sacked the Byzantine capital?

How did Geoffrey de Charny come into possession of the cloth that was exhibited in Lirey around 1355?

Was this the same shroud as the one exhibited in Turin?

There were no good answers. But there were some good circumstantial indicators.

In 1389, as we have mentioned, Pope Clement VII had given permission for another Geoffrey de Charny to exhibit "a semblance or representation of the *sudarium* of our Lord."[19]

That was either a cautious disclaimer by the papacy or the Pope knew something that he did not want clearly spelled out. But the indication is that the shroud exhibited under the authority of the so-called Anti-Pope and King Charles VI was not authentic.

The fight continued with such severity that in 1390 Clement VII yielded to the pressures and issued three statements on the subject. These indicated that while "discreet" showing of the relic was to be allowed, it was also to be proclaimed that the shroud was "not the true shroud of our Lord, but a painting or picture made in the semblance or representation of the shroud."[20]

This seemed to quiet the turmoil until 1418 when Humbert, Count de la Roche, wrote out a receipt for some church items given into his care during a war. The receipt issued to the canons of Lirey specified that one was "the semblance or representation of the shroud of our Lord."[21]

There was a delay in returning the relics. First Humbert died; then his widow, Marguerite, daughter of the first Geoffrey de Charny, refused to surrender the items to the church.

Over a period of several years, Marguerite repeatedly was threatened by the Church but obstinately refused to give in. From her first clash with the church in 1443 until 1452, she held on to the relics. In 1449, an examination of the bills issued by Clement VI indicated that this shroud was not the true one.

Indications are that on March 22, 1452, Marguerite presented the relic to the Duke Louis I in his court at Savoy. However, there is no known documentation of this. At any rate, it ended up in the sacristy of the St. Chapelle at Chambéry, France.

And Marguerite? Although excommunicated, she died without ever returning the relic or paying for the shroud.

The clergy tried to regain their relic from the Duke of Savoy. But it has remained in the possession of this house from 1452 until the present.

It has survived several accidents. On December 4, 1532, fire destroyed the church sacristy at the St. Chapelle of Chambéry. A couple of Franciscan priests and some laymen saved the shroud, but it had suffered some damage. Fire had melted the silver on the casket. The laymen, Filippo Lambert and Guglielmo Pussod, with the unidentified priests rescued the shroud, but it sustained burn holes through 48 folds. Water stains caused by extinguishing the flames also marred the relic.

The nuns of Ste. Claire patched the holes in 1543, after which it maintained a rather secluded existence until Pia's photographs unleashed a storm of discussion.

Since 1578, the shroud has remained at the Cathedral of St. John the Baptist in Turin. It reposes in a special chapel designed in 1578. In 1978, millions of people came to Turin for a public exhibition of the relic.

Many believed it was genuine. Others doubted. And by then, the finest scientific minds in the western world had focused their attention on the relic with one question in mind: Was it a hoax or genuine?

Their findings have provided us with strange new clues about the historic Jesus.

15

TESTIMONY FROM A 2,000-YEAR-OLD CLOTH

Modern scientists in pursuit of a 2,000-year-old mystery have turned up more evidence about the crucifixion of Jesus of Nazareth than anyone would have imagined. And out of those findings have come more controversies.

Dr. Pierre Barbet, a noted pathologist at St. Joseph's hospital in Paris, began his research into the shroud question with a scientist's questioning mind. He ended with a firm conviction that the shroud was genuine.

Using cadavers from the hospital, he confirmed that it was impossible for his palms to support a crucified man. The nails had to be driven through the Destot's Space in the base of the wrist. There, four bones form a tiny square which a penetrating nail would move aside without breaking a bone. The damage to one nerve, however, would be so severe that it would result in incredible pain.

The same kind of investigation indicated that the Linksfrank Space in the foot would be ideal to hold a man's extremities in place during crucifixion. The left foot was placed over the right and one nail was used, as Dr. Barbet learned from the shroud image.

He believed the victims died of asphyxia and that the bodies turned blue before death. The corpse would be completely rigid from tetanus even before rigor mortis set in.

Other researchers disputed the French pathologist's claim of asphyxia as the cause of death from crucifixion, but torture documentation from Adolf Hitler's concentration camps disclosed supporting evidence. Suspension by the wrists and the feet without any support caused the victims to perspire heavily, suffer incredible abdominal and chest cramps or spasms, and turn blue from lack of oxygen.

Not since Constantine I outlawed crucifixion around 312 AD had anything approached the inhuman tortures of the cross; but some of those which Hitler's henchmen recorded are similar.

But the question Yves Delage asked in the first hearing on the shroud at the turn of the century kept returning to challenge researchers: "How was the image made?"

Paul Vignon had favored a "vaporgraph" theory which suggested that vapors from Jesus' body had caused the image. Later investigation rendered this thesis apparently untenable.

Ray Rogers, a physical chemist at Los Alamos, New Mexico, touched on this theory along with two others in an interview[1] about how the image might have been created.

Rogers explained that Bishop Henri de Poitiers had claimed the image was a painting. His successor, Pierre d'Arcis, had claimed that de Poitiers had said it was a painting.

The second theory was that the image was produced by direct contact with the body or something of that sort.

The third hypothesis was that vapors or liquid products from the decaying body entered into a chemical reaction with the cloth.

The fourth hypothesis is that the image is the

result of some kind of heating or scorching phenomenon.

Rogers pointed out that the 1532 fire had not changed the color or total density of the scorched area. Water used to extinguish the fire had "migrated through the clothing and nothing in the image moved with the water. This says that chemically there cannot presume to be any of the kind of painting pigments, vehicles or media that would have been available to a forger before 1350 in that nothing was produced by, or used, that could have been water soluble."

The physical chemist said this ruled out the possibility that the image had been painted.

The vapor hypothesis was rejected by Rogers because the image is comprised of many little individual dots of color. These are not connected, as they would have to be if the material had to fuse or percolate by capillary flow into the cloth.

"Strangely enough," Rogers continued, "the only hypothesis that's left at the moment, or the most likely one at the moment, is that the image could be the result of some kind of a heating, scorching phenomenon."

Ray Rogers concluded that he thought the image was formed as a result of some kind of heating or scorching phenomenon.

To find out more about this, we spoke to the British author and journalist, Geoffrey Ashe.[2] Ashe told us the following:

> A human body would not be hot enough to actually scorch a cloth. What we can say is that the body of Christ could have formed that image if something extraordinary had happened to it so that it had released a burst of radiation, creating a scorching effect on the cloth.
>
> Now, of course, this does not happen to human bodies in the ordinary course of events, but according to Christian doctrine, something extraordinary did happen to this particular body.

By some process we cannot understand, it came to life again at the resurrection, so perhaps that miraculous change could have released a burst of radiation which marked the cloth, but here we are getting into something where science must be silent.

We can only say on the basis of our experiments the shroud could be as it is if it once wrapped a human body to which something extraordinary happened.

The famed London photographer, Vala,[8] has been involved for years in various innovative processes: three-dimensional, frontal projection situations and others which involve formation-like images.

He told us:

It is my opinion that the images contained in the Holy Shroud of Turin are unquestionably photographic negatives. It is quite inconceivable that anybody in the fourteenth century—which we know the shroud was historically, authentically dated back to, could have even known what a negative was—let alone produce one.

Vala explained that he had worked to achieve a three-dimensional impression of the shroud's image. He projected the face on the shroud into a completely three-dimensional solid screen. He photographed the results from many angles. The result was an in-depth profile of the figure in which the shape of the brow and the nose, as well as actual facial damage, were visible.

What did this prove to Vala about the shroud?

"I have tried very hard to actually produce a similar image on the cloth that is contained in the Shroud of Turin—and I found it quite impossible."

The famed photographer concluded, "I can say quite categorically: I don't know anybody, no matter how much photographic knowledge they have—who knows how to produce a similar image on the cloth by a photographic means."

And so the puzzle remains unsolved.

It is possible that it may never be known how the image got onto the shroud; yet there is no denying that it is there.

However, a more important question would surely be whether this shroud is the one in which Jesus was buried. Thousands of people were crucified in Jerusalem about the time of Jesus. Is there any way to prove that the Shroud of Turin has the image of Jesus?

Professor James Cameron,[4] a Scotland Yard pathologist and a professor of forensic medicine, was asked what his examination of the shroud revealed. He replied the following:

> Suffice it to say that I am satisfied that it is a photograph or image of a man—probably in the region of 35—who was flagellated before the crucifixion . . . developed rigor on the cross and was dead on the cross before being taken down. He was placed in this cloth in a state of rigor. The only part of the muscle or rigor that was broken down was in the shoulder joints.
>
> It is obvious that this man has suffered pain, and suffered considerable pain.

Could Professor Cameron elaborate on the process of whipping and crucifixion as evidenced on this image?

> If it were a Roman that was being flagellated, they would have been whipped with a cane or rod. If it was a non-Roman, probably 40 strokes were given.

The New Testament does not tell how many strokes were given Jesus in the scourging. Professor Cameron explained:

But with a Jew, it could be anything up to 120 or more strokes. In this particular shot [of the shroud], it has been calculated there are marks of 120 lashes.

The pathologist for one of the world's most famous detective agencies pointed out that on the shroud image there are marks on the head which could have come from the crown of thorns. . . . Scalp marks around the head and over the top of the head would strongly suggest that a ringlet of thorns, depicted by medieval artists and others over the years, is not, in fact, true.

Professor Cameron said that the image on the shroud had apparently worn a crown of thorns over the top and around the head. Cameron felt this was more in keeping with the Gospels that Jesus had been crowned King of the Jews.

The Scotland Yard pathologist added information not generally known to the public but common knowledge among shroud researchers:

It was common practice when one was crucified that one had to carry some part of the cross to the place of execution. This usually took the form of carrying the *patibulum,* or crossbeam of the cross.

The victim did not carry the entire cross. Dr. Pierre Barbet's calculations were to the effect that the man in the shroud had carried a crossbeam weighing about 80 pounds.

Professor Cameron continued:

With a right-handed person, with a heavy crossbeam tied to the arms, fully stretched, it is more common for the right arm to carry the weight, and therefore be lower than the left. When doing this, one would cause bruising high upon the right shoulder blade and lower down on the left.

The Scriptures do not indicate whether Jesus was right- or left-handed. Neither do they clarify why his crossbeam was given to Simon of Cyrene, although logic dictates that it had to be for a physical reason. Professor Cameron had some thoughts on that point:

> If one was walking and being pushed and shoved, one would automatically possibly fall more onto the left knee and the left forehead. It is surprising that one can see an abrasion on the left forehead, swelling on the left cheek, bruising on the upper right lip. There is also an abrasion over the left knee. All of this can be seen on the image of the shroud.

The Gospels do not say exactly where Jesus was struck, but there are indications he was hit many times. It is logical to assume at least some of those blows were to his face while he was bound and helpless.

The Scotland Yard associate had some explanations about where the nails were driven into the crucified person. His conclusions agreed with the French pathologist, Dr. Barbet.

Pathologist Cameron continued:

> One realizes that for a person who was crucified in the first hundred years AD, there was no heel bar. In other words, there was no bar underneath the heel of the foot to keep the foot from sliding down.
>
> There was no perineal bar—in other words, a bar through the crotch upon which the person who is being crucified could slide down. Therefore, he would have to be suspended by the nail through his feet or through his heel. But in this image, it is obviously through the feet.

Professor Cameron explained about the nailing of the hands:

> If the nail was through the palm of the hand and the body was suspended on the hand, there were only the minor ligaments between the fingers. The nail would quickly slip through. But if the nail was through the wrist and the multiple bones of the wrist, it would have to fall through the whole of the hand—and it would be impossible.

Although artists for centuries have depicted the nails through Jesus' palms, this is medically impossible, as both pathologists Barbet and Cameron agree. The clue to the wrist nailings had come in researching the authenticity of the shroud image where, as Professor Cameron declared, "in this particular image . . . it is through the wrist."

A curious medical fact about the shroud image was that no thumb is visible although the hand and fingers are. Dr. Barbet's experiments with cadavers had provided a medical reason for this, with which Professor Cameron concurs.

Not only was it impossible for the body of the crucified to pull through the flesh if nailed through the wrist, but the nail "would also damage the medium nerve and would cause the thumb to fold in towards the hand."

Dr. Barbet's repeated experiments with nailing a cadaver through the wrist where the medium nerves are located always caused the thumbs to involuntarily jerk into the palm.

Pathologist Cameron pointed out that "this had caused what is called a medium palsy, by bringing the thumb over."

The Scotland Yard associate discussed the alleged bloodstains on the shroud image showing the angle as flowing at 65 and 55 degrees. He said that these calculations are consistent with measurements made where a person pulls himself up and then relaxes while the foot is in a fixed position.

Professor Cameron sees a medical basis in the Gospel report of "blood and water" coming out of Jesus' side when he was pierced by a soldier's lance or spear. Crucified persons, he said, would "naturally die of respiratory failure. They collect fluid in their chest cavity. That's known as a pleural effusion."

If one were dead or dying, the professor added, and if the spear was inserted in an upward and inward direction from about a distance of eight feet, the liquid would drain out.

Dr. Barbet had earlier been convinced that the blood and water described by Saint John had corresponded to this phenomenon.

Does Professor Cameron believe the shroud is genuine?

> I do not believe that anybody, after about the time of the finding of this cloth and the beginning of the fourteenth century—that there would be anybody with enough know-how of the anatomical and the photographic, painting or forging ability to be able to forge this shroud that could have lasted to this day.

Max Frei, a renowned Swiss criminologist, has worked with pollen fossils from a small sampling of the Shroud of Turin. He has found that some of these could only have come from Jerusalem. His other findings show that the relic has also been in Constantinople.

Scientific tests making use of the finest modern technology and under supervision by the best minds have failed to nullify the possibility that the Shroud of Turin may be the actual burial sheet of Jesus.

The age of the cloth is not a major factor, since some Egyptian linens are carbon-dated as being 4,000 years old. No carbon 14 dating has been made on the shroud because the tests require destruction of a sizable portion of the item. Church officials are naturally reluctant to destroy any portion of their most priceless relic.

So the questions remain unsettled about whether the Shroud of Turin is the burial cloth of Jesus.

It must be concluded that, at this point, the Shroud of Turin can neither be proven nor disproven to be the last physical piece of evidence existing which testifies to the historic Jesus.

But the search does not end with this relic.

We turn our steps away from the Shroud of Turin to pursue a series of curious clues which lead us to the Americas in our search for the historic Jesus.

16

COULD JESUS HAVE VISITED THE AMERICAS?

Jesus of Nazareth was reportedly seen by upwards of 500 people after his resurrection. The Gospels record several specific witnesses, including his disciples, to whom Jesus appeared in rooms that had been locked for fear of persecution. Jesus simply was there, in their midst.

On the first such occasion, the disciple Thomas was absent. He refused to believe his ten fellow apostles had seen the risen Jesus. His attitude led to the term, "doubting Thomas."

> Unless I shall see in his hands the imprint of the nails, and put my finger into the place of the nails, and put my hand into his side, I will not believe. (John 20:25)

Eight days later, John tells us, Thomas was with the other disciples when the risen Jesus suddenly appeared in their midst, although the doors were shut.

"Reach here your finger," Jesus told Thomas, *"and see my hands; and reach here your hand, and put it into*

my side, and be not unbelieving, but believing." (John 20:27)

Thomas' response was one of total submission. "My Lord and my God!" (John 20:28)

Jesus asked, *"Because you have seen me, have you believed? Blessed are they who did not see, and yet believed."* (John 20:26–29)

Jesus' post-resurrection appearances in the New Testament clearly demonstrate that he could suddenly manifest himself in a closed room. Yet he could apparently be seen and touched as a physical being, even to the wounds of his crucifixion.

These are important scriptural considerations as we prepare to turn to a land far distant from Jerusalem in our search for the historical Jesus. For there are strange stories in other cultures about a white, bearded god who bears a striking similarity to Jesus of Nazareth.

Those who believe that Jesus did, indeed, appear on the American continent cite a New Testament verse that suggests this was his intent.

In his analogies, Jesus often referred to sheep. He said, for example, that he was "sent only to the lost sheep of the house of Israel." (Matthew 10:6) He repeatedly stressed his mission to the Jews, yet he helped Gentiles, such as the Roman centurion who had a sick servant and a questioning woman of Samaria, a country with which Jews had no dealings. There is historical evidence to suggest the new faith would have died if it had not spread beyond Jerusalem. But under Paul of Tarsus, a Jew who considered himself appointed by Jesus to reach the Gentiles with the message of the crucified and risen Jesus, the new sect spread beyond the Jews to the known world.

But what about the unknown world?

In Jesus' day, no one had sailed to the Americas or the Pacific Islands.

Yet, when the first white men landed in Mexico and what is now the Hawaiian Islands, the natives hailed their visitors as their returned white god who had walked among their ancestors, left mysteriously, and yet—as Jesus had in Jerusalem—promised to return.

And so we pursue these curious coincidences with a question: Could Jesus' post-resurrection appearances have given rise to the ancient American and Pacific myths about a white, bearded god who had taught many concepts similar to those of Christianity and had promised to return?

Christians today believe that Jesus will come again. They base their expectations on the New Testament.

Jesus had made his last post-resurrection appearance to the little band of believers. He had left them what is called "the Great Commission." Matthew records it as Jesus' final command:

> *All authority has been given to me in heaven and on earth. Go therefore and make disciples of all the nations, baptizing them in the name of the Father and the Son and the Holy Spirit, teaching them to observe all that I commanded you; and lo, I am with you always, even to the end of the age.* (Matt. 28: 18–20)

Luke's account adds that the disciples would be empowered from on high for the work they must do. Then Jesus led them to Bethany, the village of Mary, Martha, and Lazarus on the side of the Mount of Olives.

"He lifted up his hands and blessed them. And it came about that while he was blessing them, he parted from them. And they returned to Jerusalem with great joy." (Luke 24:50–51)

The four Gospels end at this point. The Book of Acts picks up the narrative. Scholars generally agree that the Gospel of Saint Luke was originally a part of Acts and that the Gentile writer, Luke the physician, was the author of both texts. Luke's second document resumes where the story of Jesus' life and ascension ends.

And after he had said these things, he was lifted up while they were looking on, and a cloud received him out of their sight.

And as they were gazing intently into the sky while he was departing, behold, two men in white clothing stood beside them and they also said, 'Men of Galilee, why do you stand looking up into the sky? This same Jesus, who has been taken up from you into heaven, will come in just the same manner as you have watched him go into heaven.' (Acts 1:9–11)

They returned to Jerusalem, we are told, and waited until they received power for their work in the form of the Holy Spirit. Then they went out and spread the Gospel ("good news") of Jesus everywhere. Eventually, these few believers conquered the entire Roman world, replacing its paganism with Christianity. Since then, Christians have spread their beliefs around the world.

These beliefs always included the promise that Jesus would come again. For hadn't Jesus himself told them that "every eye shall see him" when he returned? That promise had been made before his death. The angelic proclamation was reaffirmed at the ascension.

Jesus would come again.

But from where? The New Testament indicates he was to sit on the right hand of God until the Second Coming.

However, some people wonder if Jesus didn't also make other post-resurrection appearances which led to the white, bearded god of the Americas and Pacific, who likewise promised to return again.

Is there non-biblical documentary support of this possibility?

Some million members of the Church of Jesus Christ of Latter-Day Saints believe Jesus made a post-resurrection appearance to a people called the Nephites who lived in Meso America (Mexico and Central America). The encounter is recorded in the Book of Mormon

(Third Nephi, chapter 15, verse 21.) Jesus is reported to say: "You are they of whom I said, 'Other sheep I have which are not of this fold; them also I must bring, and they shall hear my voice; and there shall be one fold and one shepherd.'"

Mormons believe that Indians of the Americas are descendants of Hebrews who migrated to the New World in ancient times. They base this on the Book of Mormon, which is purportedly a translation of ancient records inscribed on gold plates and buried in a "time capsule" by the last survivor of a white race which once inhabited America.

There is a universal legend of a white god throughout the Americas and the Pacific Islands. From the Haida Indians in Alaska to the Incas of Peru, there is a striking similarity of myths.

The Haidas have a "fair god" atop a totem pole north of Ketchikan, Alaska. The Incas have Vera Coocha, or Kon-Tiki, well down the last land shelf of the Americas before Antarctica. How did this same type of white, bearded god become known to such ancient peoples long before the white men first recorded sighting any part of these great land masses?

Could these really be the same man:

Mexico: Quetzalcoatl, Votan and Wixepechocha?

Guatemala: Gucumatz

Peru: Viracocha, Jyustus and Kon-Tiki

Brazil: Sume

Colombia: Bochica

Polynesia: Lono, Kana or Kane, Konaloa, Wakea

Dakotah (Indians): Wakona

Algonkin Indians of America: Chee-Zoos? (Jesus?)

Navajo Indians of Southwest America: Yeh-ho-vah (Jehovah?)

Our determination to be open-minded in searching for the historic Jesus requires that we consider the remarkable similarities of Jesus of Nazareth with these myths from the New World.

Christopher Columbus first sighted the New World in 1492. He investigated some of the nearby islands before returning home. But the first Spanish *conquistador* was Hernando Cortez, the conqueror of Mexico.

He landed there in 1520 and was welcomed by the Aztecs as the long-expected white god of their ancestors. Cortez was able to more easily conquer the highly-advanced Aztecs and plunder the riches of the land because of this expectation.

Cortez marched on the Aztec capital, Tenochtitlan. The emperor, Montezuma, received the *conquistador* as the descendant of the god Quetzalcoatl.[1] Of course, the conqueror did not act like a god, but by the time the Aztecs realized this, it was too late. Cortez died in Spain.

The Polynesians also hailed James Cook as their long-expected white god, Lono. The English explorer was killed in 1778 by the natives of the Hawaiian Islands who found, as the Aztecs had, that the white god didn't behave as they had expected.[2]

In addition to the white or fair skin and bearded face attributed by the various tribes to their god, there were other physical characteristics in common.

He wore a long robe, sometimes with a border of red or black crosses on the hem.

He appeared among the various tribes in some mysterious or supernatural way, much as Jesus is recorded to have done with the disciples in the closed rooms of Jerusalem.

When his mission was finished, he disappeared or left the natives in much the same manner as he had first appeared.

Finally, he was born of a virgin.

Hubert H. Bancroft, whose voluminous histories of the Americas were written about a century ago, includes numerous references to the white god of the Americas. In an early account of Quetzalcoatl by a Spaniard named Mendieta—as recorded by Bancroft—Chimalma, the virgin, picked up a small green stone called chalchiuite. She became miraculously pregnant and gave birth to Quetzalcoatl.[3]

In a book called *Wi-Ne-Ma*, A. B. Meacham recalls that he got a Modoc Indian version of a virgin birth in a story from the woman chief by that name. The Modocs of California believe that the great spirit, Ka-moon-kum-chux, blew his breath upon a maiden and she became the mother of the Son of the Great Spirit.[4] There is a parallel in the New Testament account of Mary the mother of Jesus becoming pregnant by the Holy Spirit. The word is derived from the Latin "spiritus," meaning "breath."

Another variation on the same theme records that the father of Quetzalcoatl, Tonacatecotle, or Citinatonali, sent his ambassador to a virgin of Tulla. The resulting birth of Quetzalcoatl was "not by connection with a woman, but by his breath alone."[5]

The ancient narrative adds that "Citinatonali sent his son into the world to reform it."

The Toltecs, a prehistoric people, recorded Quetzalcoatl as a white man although various accounts call him a "feathered serpent."[6]

The white bearded god of the peoples of the ancient Americas was said to have brought a message of peace and kindness. He healed the sick, gave sight to the blind, restored speech and hearing to the deaf and dumb, and even raised the dead.

An Aztec prince, Istlitlxoxitl, in a history of his people comprised from codices which survived burning by Spanish priests, said that Quetzalcoatl first appeared after a period of darkness and destruction.

This sixteenth-century historian had something to say about the crucifixion of Jesus, as taught by the Spaniards, and the records of the Tulteccas, which was their the tribal name about that time.

> It was 166 years since they [the Spanish] had adjusted their years and times with the equinox, and 270 since the ancient ones [the native records] had been destroyed, when the sun and the moon eclipsed, and the earth trembled and the rocks broke, and many other things and signs took place, although there was no calamity whatever toward men.
> This happened in the time of *ce Calli,*

which, adjusting their count with ours, comes
to be at the same time when Christ our Lord
suffered, and they say it happened during the
first days of the year.[7]

Another remarkable similarity to the many apparent coincidences between Jesus of the Gospels and the
white god of the ancient Americas is left by Francisco
Hernandez. He was chaplain to the Spanish governor,
Montejo II, in Yucatan. Bartolomé de las Casas became
Bishop of Chiapas, including Yucatan. In 1545, Hernandez became the new bishop's aide. Hernandez was
sent to preach to the Mayas in the Yucatan interior.
The aide wrote de las Casas about the natives' religious
beliefs.[8] De las Casas wrote a history which survives,
Apologetica Historia de las Indias. Although written
between 1550 and 1555, it was not published until 300
years later.

De las Casas quotes Hernandez, who had met a
principal lord or chief who told the Spaniard of their
faith:

He answered him that they knew and believed in
God who was in heaven; that God was the Father, the
Son and the Holy Ghost."[9]

De las Casas continued to quote his aide's conversation with the Yucatan native.

> The Father is called by them Itzamna and
> he created man and all things. The son's name
> was Bacab, who was born from a maiden
> who had ever remained a virgin, whose name
> was Chiribirias, and who is in heaven with
> God. The Holy Spirit they called Echuac. They
> say Itzamna means 'The Great Father.'

The bishop quoted the native about Bacab, the
son who was born of a virgin. "He was killed and
lashed and a crown of thorns put on him, and he was
placed on a timber with his arms stretched out."

The Indians didn't believe that Bacab had been
nailed, but rather that he had been tied to the timber

where he died. "And he was dead for three days, and on the third day he came to life and went up to heaven, and he is there with his Father."[10]

So in about 1546, the Catholic bishop to the natives of the Americas could only comment with some awe: "If these things are true, it seems that our holy faith was known in that land. . . ."

Were the tenets of Christian faith known to the natives of interior Yucatan long before the first white man came? It was a difficult time to consider this problem because de las Casas was one of the first Roman Catholic priests to reach Central America. The bishop concluded: "These are secrets that only God knows."[11]

And so it seems today, more than 425 years since Francisco Hernandez wrote to Bishop Bartolomé de las Casas, that the Mayan Indians had known about the Trinity long before the first Spaniard landed on their shores. The Indians had known how the son was whipped, crowned with thorns, crucified, and yet resurrected after three days.

There are many other striking similarities to Christian faith throughout the Americas and across the Pacific which we found in our search for the historic Jesus. But there remain great unsolved questions:

If Jesus didn't make a post-resurrection appearance under many local names to natives of the Americas, how did these remote people have ancient traditions similar to Christian teachings and practices when the white men first landed?

Could Cortez and Cook have landed peaceably in Mexico and the then Sandwich Islands if the natives had not been expecting the white, bearded god of their ancestors to return?

How did stories so similar to those in the Gospels cross the Mediterranean to America centuries before Columbus landed as the apparently first Christian?

How, indeed!

There are no answers, but there is no doubt that there is a striking similarity between the Gospel accounts and the practices and traditions of very old

IN SEARCH OF HISTORIC JESUS

civilizations that existed in the Americas and the Pacific Islands so long ago.

And so it continues. Our search for the Jesus of history has resulted in much that is enlightening and much that is still unsettled.

Is the Shroud of Turin the last existing piece of physical evidence that Jesus of Nazareth really lived outside the Gospels?

There are strong indications that secular writers around the time of Jesus had absolutely no doubt that he lived, for there were Christians willing to die for their convictions. Suetonius, Pliny, Tacitus, and other pagan writers do not prove that Jesus actually lived, but they provide such strong circumstantial evidence that there can be no doubt these writers of antiquity believed Jesus did indeed live.

Even the Jewish *Talmud* leaves no doubt that Jesus of Nazareth lived, although its compilers took a dim view of his background and naturally do not agree with the Christian teachings.

In time, there may be more archaeological evidence or scientific confirmation of other kinds—such as records of eclipses from other cultures.

There may be records written in a strange language which have yet to see the light of day after 2,000 years, such as happened with the Dead Sea Scrolls.

But nobody knows.

It seems, somehow, that Jesus' teachings of faith are given to make us believe without any real, solid evidence outside of the Gospels.

As Jesus said to Thomas, "Blessed are they who did not see, and yet believed." (John 20:29)

After two years of research and thousands of man-hours in America and abroad, we have managed to combine the many scattered resources into what we hope is one book. We have learned more about the Jesus of the New Testament than was possible in ordinary study. We know more about the history of peoples, the legends of peoples of antiquity, and the beliefs of other religions than ever before.

We have read the chronicles of antiquity, both pagan and Judeo-Christian, in our search to know the truth.

As Pilate asked, "What is truth?"

The Gospels tell about a person called Jesus Christ who has influenced the world for 2,000 years as probably no one else ever has or will.

Yet the history of his time is strangely vague if not silent about him.

Why?

We don't know.

But faith in the Jesus of the New Testament does not depend a bit on the Jesus of history.

Neither does the Jesus of faith rest upon whether or not the Shroud of Turin is genuine or whether the myths of a white, bearded god of the Americas are based on some ancient kernel of truth, possibly involving this same Jesus.

To millions of people of all colors and races, Jesus of Nazareth lived, suffered under Pontius Pilate, was crucified, buried, and resurrected on the third day. And because Jesus lives, these millions of people believe that they too shall live again beyond the grave.

The Jesus of faith lives in the hearts of those who believe.

The Jesus of history has not yet been proven conclusively, but there is enough circumstantial evidence to suggest the fascinating search may continue.

Was Jesus of history a man or a myth? What do you think?

NOTES

CHAPTER 2

1. Quoted in D. Balsiger and C. E. Sellier, Jr., *In Search of Noah's Ark*, p. 24.

CHAPTER 3

1. Bruce, F. F., *The New Testament Documents: Are They Reliable?*

CHAPTER 5

1. L. S. Lewis, *Saint Joseph of Arimathea at Glastonbury*, pp. 53–54.
2. Lewis, p. 151.
3. Lewis, p. 152.
4. Lewis, p. 152.
5. *Urantia*, p. 1402.

CHAPTER 6

1. F. F. Bruce, "Lysanias," *The New Bible Dictionary*, p. 761.

2. D. E. Hiebert, "Lysanias," *The Zondervan Pictorial Encyclopedia of the Bible,* vol. 3, p. 1013.

3. Josephus, "Antiquities of the Jews," p. 382.

4. Josephus, p. 382.

CHAPTER 12

1. *Catholic Encyclopedia,* vol. 13, p. 420.

2. Josephus, p. 379.

3. Josephus, p. 423.

4. Josephus, "Dissertation I: The Testimonies of Josephus Concerning Jesus Christ, John the Baptist, and James the Just Vindicated," p. 639.

5. Quoted in J. McDowell, *Evidence Demands a Verdict,* p. 85. Printed by permission. Copyright © Campus Crusade for Christ, Inc. (1972). All rights reserved.

6. McDowell, p. 84.

7. McDowell, p. 85.

8. McDowell, p. 85.

9. McDowell, p. 86.

10. McDowell, p. 87.

11. McDowell, p. 86.

12. McDowell, p. 88.

CHAPTER 13

1. Walsh, *The Shroud,* p. 96.

2. Walsh, p. 99.

3. Walsh, p. 99.

4. Walsh, p. 101.

5. Walsh, p. 50.

6. *Encyclopedia Americana,* vol. 1, p. 41.

7. R. K. Wilcox, *Shroud,* p. 93.

8. *Oxford English Dictionary,* vol. 2, p. 1713.

CHAPTER 14

1. Wilcox, pp. 79–90.

2. Wilcox, pp. 80–81.

3. Wilcox, p. 81.

4. T. Humber, *The Sacred Shroud,* p. 78.

5. E. Bradford, *The Great Betrayal*, pp. 21, 205.
6. Bradford, p. 141.
7. Bradford, p. 9.
8. Bradford, p. 20.
9. Bradford, p. 203.
10. Bradford, p. 162.
11. Bradford, p. 163.
12. R. de Clari, *The Conquest of Constantinople*, p. 214.
13. Humber, p. 97.
14. Humber, p. 97.
15. Humber, p. 101.
16. Humber, p. 110.
17. Humber, p. 110.
18. Humber, p. 98.
19. Humber, p. 97.
20. Humber, p. 100.
21. Humber, p. 101.

CHAPTER 15

1. Interview with Ray Rogers, Los Alamos, New Mexico, April 14, 1979.
2. Interview with Geoffrey Ashe, Somerset, England, April 23, 1979.
3. Interview with Leo Vala, London, England, April 25, 1979.
4. Interview with James Cameron, London, England, April 24, 1979.

CHAPTER 16

1. D. G. Brinton, *Myths of the New World*, p. 202.
2. M. E. Petersen, "The Great White God Was a Reality," *The Improvement Era*, Sept. 1969, p. 8.
3. H. H. Bancroft, *Native Races of the Pacific States of North America*, vol. 3, p. 250.
4. A. B. Meacham, *Wi-Ne-Ma*, pp. 112–123.
5. Bancroft, vol. 3, p. 272.
6. Bancroft, vol. 3, p. 273.
7. T. Ferguson, *One Fold and One Shepherd*, p. 136.

8. Ferguson, p. 139.
9. Quoted in Ferguson, p. 140.
10. Quoted in Ferguson, p. 140.
11. Ferguson, p. 140.

BIBLIOGRAPHY

BIBLES

The New American Standard Bible. The Lockman Foundation. La Habra, CA: Collins World Pub., 1975.

The New American Bible. Bishop's Committee of the Confraternity of Christian Doctrine. New York: P. J. Kenedy & Sons, 1970.

The Holy Scriptures According to the Masoretic Text, 2 vols. Philadelphia, PA: The Jewish Publication Society of America, 1977.

REFERENCE TEXTS

Catholic Encyclopedia. New York: Encyclopedia Press, Inc., 1958.

The Columbia Viking Desk Encyclopedia. New York: Viking Press, 1953.

A Dictionary of the Bible. ed. James Hastings. New York: Charles Scribner's Sons, 1903.

Encyclopedia Americana. New York: Americana Corp., 1966.

Encyclopedia Biblica. New York: Macmillan Co., 1901.

Everyman's Atlas of Ancient and Classical Geography. New York: J. M. Dent & Sons, 1975.

Harper's Encyclopedia of Bible Life. New York: Harper & Row, 1978.

Hebrew-English Lexicon. Grand Rapids, MI: Zondervan Publishing, 1976.
Oxford English Dictionary, 2 vols. New York: Oxford University Press, 1971.

GENERAL REFERENCES

Albright, William F. "The Eliminating of King 'So,' " *The Bulletin of the American Schools of Oriental Research.* No. 171. Oct. 1963. p. 66.

Allegro, John. *The Dead Sea Scrolls.* Gretna, LA: Pelican Books, 1956.

Ballou, Robert O. *The Other Jesus.* New York: Doubleday, 1972.

Balsiger, David & Charles E. Sellier, Jr. *In Search of Noah's Ark.* CA: Sun Classic Pictures, Inc., 1976.

Bancroft, Hubert H. *Native Races of the Pacific States of North America.* New York: D. Appleton & Co., 1876.

Barbet, Pierre. *A Doctor at Calvary,* trans. Earl of Wicklow. New York: Image Books, 1963.

Barclay, William. *Jesus As They Saw Him.* Grand Rapids, MI: William B. Eerdmans, 1962.

Berkhof, Hendrikus. *Christ and the Meaning of History.* Atlanta, GA: John Knox Press, 1966.

Bierhorst, John, ed. and trans. *Black Rainbow: Legends of the Incas and Myths of Ancient Peru.* New York: Farrar, Straus & Giroux, 1976.

Bradford, Ernle. *The Great Betrayal.* London: Hodder & Stoughton, 1967.

Briggs, Lawson. "Icon Supreme?" *The Plain Truth,* Dec. 1978.

Brinton, Daniel G. *Myths of the New World.* Blauvelt, NY: Multimedia Publishing Corp., 1976.

———. *Myths of the Americas.* Blauvelt, NY: Multimedia Publishing Corp., 1976.

Brown, Raymond E. *The Birth of the Messiah.* New York: Doubleday, 1977.

Bruce, F. F. "Lysanias," *The New Bible Dictionary,* ed. J. D. Douglas. Grand Rapids, MI: William B. Eerdmans, 1979.

Cambell, W. A. *Did the Jews Kill Jesus?* New York: Peter Eckler Co., 1927.

Cheshire, G. L. *Pilgrimage to the Shroud.* New York: McGraw-Hill, 1956.

Conzelmann, Hans. *History of Primitive Christianity,* trans. John E. Steely. New York: Abingdon Press, 1965.

Craveri, Marcello. *The Life of Jesus.* New York: Grove Press, 1967.

The Crucifixion by an Eye Witness. Supplemental Harmonic Series, vol. II, 4th ed. Chicago: Indo-American Book Co., 1911.

Dart, John. *The Laughing Savior.* New York: Harper and Row, 1970.

De Clari, Robert. *The Conquest of Constantinople,* trans. E. H. McNeal. New York: Columbia University Press, 1936.

Dimont, Max L. *Jews, God, and History.* New York: Signet, 1962.

Duffield, Guy P. *Handbook of Bible Lands.* Glendale, CA: G/L Regal Books, 1969.

Dobson, Rev. C. C. *Did Our Lord Visit Britain As They Say?* England: Covenant Publishing, 1974.

Durant, Will. *The Story of Civilization.* New York: Simon & Schuster, 1944.

Enelow, H. G. *A Jewish View of Jesus.* New York: Bloch Publishing, 1931.

Emerson, William A., Jr. *The Jesus Story.* New York: Harper and Row, 1960.

Faber-Kaiser, A. *Jesus Died in Kashmir.* London: Gordon & Cremonesi, 1977.

Fox, Langton D. *The Holy Shroud.* London: Catholic Truth Society, 1975.

Foster, Harry. *Speaking Anonymously.* USA: Christian Literature Crusade, 1973.

Ferguson, Thomas S. *One Fold and One Shepherd.* San Francisco, CA: Books of California, 1958.

Gibbon, Edward. *The Decline and Fall of the Roman Empire,* 3 vols. New York: E. P. Dutton & Co., 1962.

Ginzberg, Louis. *The Legends of the Jews.* New York: Simon & Schuster, 1953.

Goetz, Delia & Sylvannus G. Morley, trans. *Popul Vuh.* Norman, OK: University of Oklahoma Press, 1950.

Goldstein, Morris. *Jesus in the Jewish Tradition.* New York: Macmillan Co., 1950.

Gorman, Ralph. *The Last Hours of Jesus.* New York: Sheed & Ward, 1960.

Graetz, H. *History of the Jews.* Vol. 2. Philadelphia, PA: The Jewish Publication Society of America, 1960.

Grant, Michael. *The Twelve Caesars*. New York: Charles Scribner's Sons, 1975.

————. *Jesus: An Historian's Review of the Gospels*. New York: Charles Scribner's Sons, 1977.

Great People of the Bible and How They Lived. Pleasantville, NY: The Reader's Digest Association Inc., 1971.

Gromacki, Robert G. *New Testament Survey*. Grand Rapids, MI: Baber Book House, 1977.

Halley, Henry H. *Halley's Bible Handbook*. Grand Rapids, MI: Zondervan Publishing, 1965.

Hiebert, D. E. "Lysanias," *The Zondervan Pictorial Encyclopedia of the Bible*, ed. Merrill C. Tenney. Grand Rapids, MI: Zondervan Publishing, 1977.

Heyerdahl, Thor. *American Indians in the Pacific*. New York: Rand-McNally, 1952.

Honore, Pierre. *In Quest of the White God*, trans. Oliver Coburn & Ursula Lehrburger. New York: G. P. Putnam's Sons.

Humber, Thomas. *The Shroud of Turin*. New York: Pocket Books, 1978.

Hunter, Milton R. "Christ in America." *The Improvement Era*, June 1961, p. 408.

Hynek, R. W. *The True Likeness*. London: Sheed & Ward, 1951.

Jeremias, Joachim. *In the Time of Jesus*. Philadelphia, PA: Fortress Press, 1977.

Josephus: Complete Works, trans. William Whiston. Grand Rapids, MI: Kregel Publications, 1977.

Jowett, George F. *The Drama of the Lost Disciples*. London: Covenant Publishing Co., 1978.

Keller, Werner. *The Bible as History*, trans. William Neil. New York: William Morrow & Co., 1956.

Kenyon, Kathleen. *Royal Cities of the Old Testament*. New Yok: Schocken Books.

————. *The Bible and Recent Archaeology*. London: British Museum Publications, 1978.

Klassen, Frank R. *The Chronology of the Bible*. Glendale, CA: G/L Regal Books, 1975.

Laister, M. L. W. *The Greater Roman Historians*. San Francisco, CA: University of California Press, 1971.

Lamsa, George M. *The Hidden Years of Jesus*. St. Petersburg, FL: Aramaic Bible Society, 1973.

————. *The Man from Galilee*. New York: Doubleday, 1970.

"Laser, 'Death Ray' that Improves Life," *Reader's Digest*. Pleasantville, NY: The Reader's Digest Association, Inc., August 1978.

Levi. *The Aquarian Gospel of Jesus the Christ*. Marina Del Rey, CA: De Vorss & Co., 1907.

Lewis, Lionel Smithett. *Saint Joseph of Arimathea at Glastonbury*. Cambridge, Eng.: James Clarke & Co., Ltd., 1976.

Macalister, R. A. S. *A History of Civilization in Palestine*. Cambridge, Eng.: Oxford University Press, 1912.

Matthews, Shailer. *A History of New Testament Times in Palestine*. New York: Macmillan Co., 1913.

McDowell, Josh. *Evidence That Demands a Verdict*. San Bernardino, CA: Campus Crusade for Christ, 1972.

Meacham, A. B. *Wi-Ne-Ma*. Hartford, CT: American Publishing Co., 1876.

Miller, Madelaine S. & J. Lane Miller. *Harper's Bible Dictionary*. New York: Harper and Brothers, 1952.
———. *Encyclopedia of Bible Life*. New York: Harper and Row, 1944.

Mills, James R. *The Gospel According to Pontius Pilate*. San Francisco, CA: San Francisco Book Co., 1977.

"Mystery of the Holy Shroud." *Life Magazine*, Dec. 1978, pp. 30–34.

Nibley, Hugh. *Since Cumorah*. Salt Lake City, UT: Deseret Books, 1973.
———. *Early Accounts of Jesus' Childhood*. Salt Lake City, UT: Deseret Books, 1965.

Noerdlinger, Henry S. *Moses and Egypt*. Los Angeles, CA: University of Southern California Press, 1956.

Patriarchs: The World History of the Jewish People, 3 vols., ed. Benjamin Mazar. New Brunswick, NJ: Rutgers University Press, 1970.

Peterson, Elder Mark E. "The Great White God Was a Reality." *Improvement Era*, Sept. 1969, pp. 8–11.

Pfeiffer, Charles F. & Howard F. Vos. *The Wycliffe Historical Geography of Bible Lands*. Chicago: Moody Press, 1974.

Prime, W. C. *Holy Cross*. New York: Anson, Randolph & Co., 1877.

Radin, Max. *The Jews Among the Greeks and Romans*. Philadelphia, PA: The Jewish Publication Society of America, 1915.

Rand, Abby. *American Traveller's Guide to Israel*. New York: Scribner's, 1974.

Ricci, Giulio. *The Way of the Cross in the Light of the Holy Shroud*. New York: Centro Romano de Sindonologia, 1975.

Ridenaur, Fritz. *What's the Difference?* Glendale, CA: G/L Regal Books, 1967.

Riggs, James Stevenson. *A History of the Jewish People*. New York: Charles Scribner's Sons, 1910.

Rinaldi, Peter M. *It Is The Lord*. New York: Warner Books, Inc., 1975.

Robertson, John M. *The Historical Jesus*. London: Watts and Co., 1916.

Robinson, Preston & Christine. *Biblical Sites in the Holy Land*. Salt Lake City, UT: Deseret Books, 1963.

Roth, Cecil, *The Jewish Contribution to Civilization*. New York: Harper & Row, 1940.

Ryrie, Charles C. *The Bible: Truth Without Error*. Dallas: Dallas Theological Seminary, 1972.

Saxtorph, Niels M. *Warriors and Weapons of Early Times*. New York: Macmillan Co., 1972.

Schoeps, Hans Joachim. *The Jewish-Christian Argument*, trans. David E. Green. New York: Holt, Rinehart, and Winston, 1963.

Schonfield, Hugh. *Secrets of the Dead Sea Scrolls*. New York: Thomas Yaseloff, Inc.

———. *The Passover Plot*. New York: Bantam Books, 1970.

Schweitzer, Albert. *The Quest of the Historical Jesus*. New York: Macmillan Co., 1968.

———. *Out of My Life and Thought*. New York: Times-Mirror, 1957.

A Sculptor Interprets the Holy Shroud of Turin. New York: Mission Press, 1954.

Segal, J. B. *The Hebrew Passover*. New York: Oxford University Press, 1963.

Shearer, Tony. *Lord of the Dawn: Quetzalcoatl*. Happy Camp, CA: Naturegraph Publishers, Inc., 1971.

Shewell-Cooper, W. E. *Plants, Flowers, and Herbs of the Bible*. New Canaan, CT: Keats Publishing, Inc., 1977.

Silverman, William B. *Judaism and Christianity*. New York: Behrman House, 1968.

Slaughter, Frank G. *The Galileans*. New York: Doubleday, 1977.

Steinberg, Milton. *Basic Judaism*. New York: Harcourt, Brace & World, 1947.

Stevenson, Kenneth. *Proceedings of the 1977 United*

States Conference of Research on the Shroud of Turin. New York: Holy Shroud Guild, 1977.

Sullivan, Barbara. "How in Fact Was Jesus Christ Laid in His Tomb?" *National Review*, July 20, 1973, pp. 785–789.

Taylor, John W. *The Coming of the Saints*. London: Covenant Publishing Co., Ltd., 1969.

Tenney, Merrill C. *New Testament Times*. Grand Rapids, MI: William B. Eerdmans Co., 1975.

Terrien, Samuel. *The Golden Bible Atlas*. Racine, WI: Western Publishing Co., Inc., 1957.

Thomas, Michael. "The Shroud of Turin." *Rolling Stone Magazine*, Dec. 28, 1978–Jan. 11, 1979, pp. 78–84.

Trever, John. *The Untold Story of Qumran*. New York: Revell, 1956.

Urantia. Chicago: Urantia Foundation, 1955.

Van Der Ploeg, J. *The Excavations at Qumran*, trans. Kevin Smyth. New York: Longmans, Green and Co., 1958.

Vignon, Paul. *The Shroud of Christ*. Westminster, Eng.: Archibald, Constable & Co., 1902.

Walker, Williston. *History of the Christian Church*. New York: Charles Scribner's Sons, 1945.

Wallace, Irving. *The Word*. New York: Simon and Schuster, 1972.

Walsh, John. *The Shroud*. New York: Random House, 1963.

Wight, Fred H. *Manners and Customs of Bible Lands*. Chicago: Moody Press, 1976.

Wilcox, Robert K. *Shroud*. New York: Bantam Books, 1977.

Williamson, G. A. *The World of Josephus*. New York: Little Brown & Co., 1964.

Wilson, Ian. *The Shroud of Turin*. New York: Doubleday, 1978.

———. "The Shroud of Turin and the Resurrection." *Sign*, April 1978, pp. 35–41.

Wolf, Betty Hartman. *Journey Through the Holy Land*. New York: Doubleday, 1967.

Woodward, Kenneth L. & Christopher Matthews. "Christ's Shroud?" *Newsweek Magazine*, Sept. 18, 1978, p. 95.

Wouk, Herman. *This Is My God*. New York: Doubleday, 1959.

Wuenschel, Rev. Edward. *The Holy Shroud of Turin.* New York: Holy Shroud Guild, 1953.

———. *Self-Portrait of Christ.* New York: Holy Shroud Guild, 1957.

ABOUT THE AUTHORS

CHARLES E. SELLIER, JR. performs the multiple duties of executive, producer, and writer for one of the most active and successful production and distribution companies in today's film industry. As President, both for the Production Company, Schick Sunn Classic Productions, and its distribution subsidiary company, Sunn Classic Pictures, Sellier restricts his productions only to films suitable for the family viewing audience.

Sellier has authored such books as *The Lincoln Conspiracy, The Life and Times of Grizzly Adams,* and *In Search of Noah's Ark*—all were followed by successful film productions produced by him. In his 19 year filmmaking career, he has also produced many other theatrical films including *Beyond and Back, The Brothers O'Toole, The Bermuda Triangle, The Fall of the House of Usher, Mountainman, The Outer Space Connection, The Mysterious Monsters,* and *In Search of Historic Jesus.*

Dividing his writing and theatrical film production activities with television programming producton, Sellier, with typical enthusiasm, created and produced the Classics Illustrated series of two hour special films for N.B.C. which included the classic stories, *The Last of the Mohicans, The Time Machine, The Deerslayer,* and *The Incredible Rocky Mountain Race.* He has also produced and created the popular *Grizzly Adams, Mark Twain's America,* and *Greatest Heroes of the Bible* series.

Sellier makes his home in the historic silver mining town and now renowned skiing area of Park City, Utah in the rugged Wasatch mountain range.

LEE RODDY was born on an Illinois farm, but grew up on a small California ranch. He began writing at age 14. At 23, he went to Hollywood to complete his college degree and write professionally. He has been a staff writer-researcher for a book publisher plus producer of theatrical films and network television programs. In addition, he has been a broadcast station manager, newspaper editor and publisher, public relations executive, advertising agency promotion director and full-time professional freelance writer.

He used his lifelong interest in history to author, cowrite or ghost write more than twenty books during the last five years. Two were secular bestsellers; one was a Christian bestseller. Following what he calls a "born again" experience, Lee Roddy turned his writing toward religious subjects. Several of his books have been nonfiction Christian biographies or self-help paperbacks. He has five novels coming out with a religious theme. Five of his books are tied in with motion pictures.

He and his wife, Cicely, have made their home in Salt Lake City, Utah, for the past two years. They have a married son and daughter in California.